Because I Love You

: My DTS Story

Author HeeJin Han Kimjacobs
English Translator Eunice & Rachel Joung
Artist Jiyeon Lee

YA Yeosu
YWAM AIIM Yeosu

Reading through this unique and exciting book brought back memories of my own DTS several decades earlier. Heejin describes a life-changing experience by sharing with us simple stories of how God turned her life around through the relationships with students and teachers. It reads like a private diary, but it results in a dynamic transformation of her life, her relationship with her husband, and above with her Lord.

Rev. David Ross
Missionary to South Korea from U.S.A
Founder of Youth With A Mission(YWAM) Korea
Founder of YWAM Antioch Institute for International Mission(AIIM)

As Heejin's DTS school leader, I am deeply honoured and blessed to witness her transformative journey now captured so vividly in this book. Her testimony reflects the profound ways God works through individuals during a Discipleship Training School, showing how He shapes hearts, relationships, and futures. While every person's path may differ, Heejin's story provides a compelling and inspiring glimpse into the realities of short-term missions and the power of YWAM's faith-based training programs. I wholeheartedly recommend this book to anyone considering a step into missions or simply desiring to see how God's grace can change a life.

Bruno Loyiso
Previous Director of YWAM Worcester, South Africa
Author of "A More Desirable Way"
& "Reforming Worcester, South Africa"

Introduction

In 2005, I joined my church's medical mission team and went overseas to serve for 5-6 days. I thought this was enough as a Christian for the kingdom of the Lord. But God! He had so much more for me than I had ever expected or imagined. This book contains my stories of completing a Discipleship Training School (DTS) with Youth With A Mission (YWAM) and the events that occurred thereafter. As a city girl accustomed to the convenience of metropolitan life, a gourmet who desires delicious and delectable delights, and a luxury-lover, I experienced missions training with DTS that was here and there and beyond my imagination. I decided to let go of my embarrassment and open my story to the public. It's the story of a missionary trip that would have been impossible without God's grace and love.

I write from a combination of my diaries, DTS lecture notes, one-on-one homework, and memories. I was able to work filled with grace and joy because of the memories that came back to me, the emotions I felt again, and new perspectives of events. I hope this book can be of help to those who are curious about DTS and short-term missions. Even though many things may be lacking in my sharing of my experiences and emotions, please look over this account graciously. Together with the readers, I would like to encourage and support those in ministry who are working hard all over the world for the kingdom of God. Thank you! You can do it !

Through the DTS and the Vision Trip, I felt God's grace deeply, and I wrote this book with gratitude to God for giving me such great opportunities. I started writing this account in South Korea in May 2019, and it took about 100 days to write the first draft. After reading it, Casablanca started interceding, and artist Jiyeon Lee drew pictures. Dreaming of an English version, I used Google Translate to translate my writing, but it was a clumsy translation that was difficult for my Korean-American husband, who knows some Korean, to even read a page properly.

In the meantime, under the guidance of the Lord, I came to the YWAM Pneuma Springs (It means Fountain of the Holy Spirit) in Seattle, USA. The Lord blessed me with a beautiful meeting there, so from December 14, 2020, I started working on the English translation with Rachel Joung. She had just come from DTS in Honolulu, Hawaii. While Rachel was studying at the School of Biblical Studies (SBS), her older sister Eunice Joung, who returned from SBS, took over the baton and started working where Rachel had left off. This book was able to be published in English thanks to meeting these sisters in the U.S.A, which was unexpected, and their talent and their deep love for the Lord. Dream Team Jiwon, a graphic designer, willingly volunteered to draw maps for us. This writing is the fruit of the cooperation of many people who love God. I love and appreciate everyone. Thank you very much.

I am thankful for *Pilgrim's Progress* (Edited by C.J. Lovik, Illustrated by Mike Wimmer), which helped me awaken to hear the voice of the Lord to go do the DTS. I would like to thank Senior Pastor Jaehoon Lee of Onnuri Church for his sermons that helped me discern the will of the Lord. I give my love and respect to the South African Worcester Base DTS staff and instructors, who helped me feel the love of the Lord in my heart. I would like to thank YWAM Pneuma Springs for giving me the opportunity and love to serve God by praying, worshiping, and serving God together. Thank you very much.

I am deeply grateful to my sisters in Christ and friends who have helped me so far. When I was weak and unable to stand alone, I could grow in faith through the patience and love of those whom the Lord sent. Special respect is given to my grandmother Aesun Kim and my mother-in-law Esther Lee. I miss my grandmother, my example of faith. Thank you, Mother-in-law. She encouraged me and wrote in my prayer letter, "I love you. Your writing reaches my heart." I believe they are still supporting me in Heaven. I express my gratitude and respect to my parents who gave birth to me and raised me. I also would like to express my gratitude to my younger brother who supported and prayed for me to do DTS. I express my deep love and gratitude to my husband, Joshua, who loved and supported me so that I could feel the love of the Lord from my head to my heart.

Lord... Thank you for holding me in a kind and gentle way so that I can write this book without giving up until the end. I give thanks and glory to the Lord who will lead me with unchanging love yesterday, today, and forever.

Tomatoes symbolize kindness and gentleness (A to Z Dream Symbology Dictionary, Dr Barbie Breathitt). I hope that God's kind and gentle caring love will be delivered to you through this book. I give thanks to God who supports us today with love that is bright, fresh and abundant like tomatoes.

CONTENTS

PART I. START

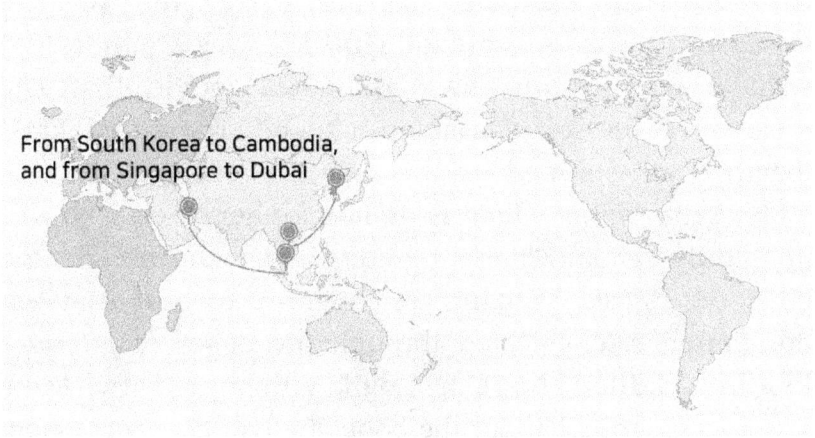

From South Korea to Cambodia, and from Singapore to Dubai

CHAPTER 1

Awake!

"Heejin, let's drop by the bookstore real quick." One morning in December of 2012, I had just finished a special early morning prayer meeting. After the service, Casablanca (This is a pseudonym. She was so impressed with a scene from the Casablanca movie that she nicknamed herself Casablanca.) and I ate breakfast together and stopped by the church bookstore. She was looking for *Pilgrim's Progress* to buy for her niece, who was in middle school(7th to 9th grade). After she bought the book, we started drinking coffee with a friend we met at the church café. I leafed through the pages of *Pilgrim's Progress* (Edited by C.J. Lovik, Illustrated by Mike Wimmer), curious about the book she had chosen. "Oooo, nice drawing..." The sound of the two friends' conversation grew distant, as I started reading the book.

Until now, I had tried to read *Pilgrim's Progress* several times, but the writing style was old so that I didn't turn a single page and gave up reading. And the book went directly back onto the bookshelf. But what was this?! I actually liked the pictures, and I had to admit that the book was a fun read. After saying good-bye to Casablanca and leaving the café, I couldn't stop thinking about the next chapter of the book! *You know what? I should just buy one, too.* I began to read *Pilgrim's Progress* at work and at home and in a few days, tore through the book from beginning to end. Unlike with other books, however, indescribable joy remained even after I finished *Pilgrim's Progress*. The phrase "stay awake" from the book continued to reverberate in my head. A few days later, I went to a bookstore and bought all their copies of *Pilgrim's Progress* left on the bookshelf. Then I gave a copy to my brother Daehwi saying, "You should read this," and to my coworker asking, "Have you ever read the book *Pilgrim's Progress*? You need to check it out." I passed the books out to my fellow coworkers, friends, and family.

Meanwhile, at my church, the 35th day of a special 40 days of prayer arrived on January 24, 2013, about a month after God started stirring in me the message to "stay awake." The text of that morning's sermon was Genesis 13, where Abram parts with Lot. As they go their separate ways, Abram gives Lot the first choice, telling him to choose which land he wants. Paster made a comment that I didn't usually hear in relation to this passage.

"In giving Lot the first choice, Abraham was giving precedent to his family and forgetting God's covenant in the land of Canaan." I thought, *Isn't consideration for our family a good thing?! Hmmm... What if Abram had left Lot in Haran? Would Lot have stayed out of Sodom? Then it was really bad for Lot that Abram went with him out of familial love and duty. Wouldn't it be bad if I made my parents and brother the reason I didn't go to Discipleship Training School (DTS)? Would it cause loss for my parents and my brother later? God! Is there anything I need to change inside of me? If so, what is it?* I prayed as I listened.

The sermon led me to reflect on my duty to my family. When I was young, my family was poor, and I was able to become a doctor because of my parents' dedicated sacrifice. Pleasing my parents and repaying them was important to me. A conflict broke out in my heart all day as thoughts swirled in my head. *Is DTS an excuse to avoid my responsibility to my family? Or, like Abram, are we to leave Ur of the Chaldeans?*

At the beginning of the next day's sermon, the pastor again said that Abram's consideration and responsibility for Lot were human thoughts against God's covenant. I talked to my friends Casablanca and Sungeun and asked for intercession concerning the future. And during Quiet Time (QT same as morning devotion), I thought, *I need to step out with courage and go do my DTS.*

That night, I took the opportunity to talk to my husband Joshua. "Let's go and do our DTS!" My husband froze in place. The first words out of his mouth were, "I was going to go and buy the Retona in Incheon this weekend." At the time, my husband and I were obsessed with buying a used Kia Retona. My husband listened to my reasons for going to DTS and said, "I had just finished thinking through our 10-year plan. I like the idea of going to DTS, but it's not easy… I will pray about it." To say the least, he reacted to my abrupt announcement like a gentleman.

Before I continue, I want to explain DTS for a moment. DTS (Discipleship Training School) is YWAM's primary discipleship training program. An international and interdenominational missions organization, YWAM (Youth With A Mission) was founded in 1960 by Loren Cunningham with the aim of raising up and sending all generations dedicated to Jesus Christ to effectively spread the gospel to all nations. DTS lasts about five to six months, with the training coming in two parts. During the lecture phase, students focus on knowing God, His Word, and His world. Then during the outreach phase, students break up into teams to serve God out in the world through caring for people and sharing the good news of Jesus.

So community living is an essential part of DTS! As a stubborn city girl, I took personal privacy very seriously. Even before we got married, my husband had told me that going to DTS was a family tradition. My response at that time was, "Don't we have to live in community if we do DTS?! Going abroad for a week-long mission trip is enough for me. I can't imagine community life. It really doesn't suit me." After hearing my strong opinion on the matter, my husband didn't say anything more about DTS. And by the end of our second year of marriage, Joshua had made his own long-term plan for the next ten years - buying the car he wanted (that good ol' Kia Retona), getting promoted at work ... But one day, out of the blue, his wife says to him, "Should we go to DTS?" Looking back, I was lucky we were still in the honeymoon phase. No matter what I did, I was still lovely~

From the very next day, we worshiped and spent time in the Word to seek the Lord's will. My husband even canceled his birthday trip plans. After the early morning service, we read Genesis 13:14-17. "Look around from where you are, to the north and south, to the east and west ... Go, walk through the length and breadth of the land." In the meantime, my thoughts moved from anxiety to conviction, and the idea that going to DTS was the Lord's will grew more and more solid. And so after QT on the morning of February 14, twenty days after I mentioned DTS, Joshua said God answered him with Genesis 24:50, "This is from the LORD..."

Then one night in my dreams, I saw an unusual mountain that I had never seen before. It was a grayish brown mountain with several peaks connected in a row. Then the scene panned out to an endlessly long fir forest covered in white snow and to blue skies spreading out beyond the forest. Looking at the scenery in my dream, my heart felt cool and free.

What does this dream mean? Could the scene be connected to where we will go in the future?!

Fig 2. The snow-covered firs I saw in my dream

CHAPTER 2

Go fast, Go Quickly

We felt God was telling us to go east, west, north, and south, so we expected to eventually go to a secondary YWAM school and to staff at the place He opened for us. So we planned on four to five years of long-term missions. We put our heads together and came up with the "One-Year Plan in preparation for our DTS Departure." However the Word of God came clearly to us again and again. "Go now, go fast, go quickly!" *Why was He speaking to us like this?!! We would surely prepare and leave for DTS within the upcoming year. But why the urgency?* Nevertheless, neither of us could deny this intense feeling. *Wow! So this is why missionaries go!*

We decided to sell our honeymoon house to finance our DTS. Joshua reasoned, "If it's meant to be sold, it will sell." He put the house on the market at the upper limits of the price range. He had better faith than I did. Our real estate agent questioned us. "Don't you know how bad the real estate market is these days? You don't know the market. Your house won't sell." But a mere two days later, while I was at work, my husband called. Someone who came to see our house put in an offer to buy it at the asking price, so we went in and signed the contract the next day, only three days after we put the house up for sale. Praise the Lord!

Oh well, with the house selling so unexpectedly like this, we knew we hadn't misheard God's voice. We prepared to leave for DTS in earnest. Now we had to decide where to go. Where was the right place for us? In the meantime,

God had told us to "go from your country, your people and your father's household", so we excluded Korea, where I grew up, and the US, where my husband grew up. Next, we thought about the physical state of our bodies (We were two people in our forties!), our tendencies, budget, and the time we had to prepare and leave. We had quite a lot to consider.

Joshua, who was much more familiar with DTS, began to search on the internet. He found two places. One was a Crossroads DTS in Baguio in the Philippines. Crossroads DTS (CDTS) is a DTS tailored specifically for people aged 30 and older and is open to singles, couples, and families. Joshua also discovered an Awakening DTS in Worcester, South Africa. The DTS in Baguio seemed to be a better fit since it was a Crossroads DTS, the flights to the location were cheap, and the cultures of Korea and the Philippines were more similar than the cultures of Korea and South Africa. In many ways, the Philippines seemed more suitable for us. Except for one thing...It was too close to South Korea! I thought it would be better to go to a distant place so that I couldn't run away even if I wanted to give up. My husband didn't have a problem with DTS because he had done one when he was young, but my situation was different. I had never lived in a community and had never been outside South Korea for more than a week. My taste was picky, and I hated being uncomfortable ... I knew I needed a location where I couldn't come back even if I felt like shouting, "No more!! I quit!!" So I said to my husband, "South Africa! South Africa!". Thankfully, my husband was understanding once again.

The next beast to tackle was work. I couldn't just simply

quit my job at the hospital since ending my contract early would result in a significant amount of penalties. Six months still remained in my contract. Besides, how would I explain my situation to the three directors of my company, none of whom attended church? I mustered up courage and called the head of the dermatology department. However, her response was less complicated than I had anticipated. She said she will call and ask the head director, and get back to me. Soon the answer came. She called back, reporting, "He said, 'What can I do about it? She said she's going on missions!'" With that call, I could end my contract smoothly with approval.

We were wrapping up with work and our house, and it was going well as if we were sailing in a fair wind. But the fear of an unknown future took hold of my mind like a stormy wave. *Can we really do this?!* I was really afraid. I tried to cheer myself up by doing QT, but it was not easy to shake off the fear I was feeling. Then one day, when I arranged the bookshelves, I found a book that my mother-in-law had read - Loren Cunningham's *Courage at the Edge of the Cliff*. Here and there were traces of my mother-in-law's reading with her underlined sections. Joshua and I began to read together, setting aside time to read chapter by chapter. And even when we read about serious situations, we laughed at the witty and moving stories and were able to find courage and faith once again.

After 2 weeks of hectic preparations to leave, we were tired. Around February 28, Joshua's old friends, James, his wife Priscilla, and Peter visited our house during their visit to Korea. As we had dinner together and talked, they prayed for us. Peter told us, "It's time to sail," and shared Isaiah 50:4 - "The Sovereign Lord has given me a well-instructed tongue, to know the word that sustains the weary. He wakens me morning by morning, wakens my ear to listen like one being instructed." Priscilla gave us Isaiah 12:3 - "With joy you will draw water from the wells of salvation." James said that he saw me delighted in beautiful nature that had mountains, fields, grass, and blooming flowers. And he shared Malachi 4:2 - "But for you who revere my name, the sun of righteousness will rise with healing in its rays. And you will go out and frolic like well-fed calves." Through these three people, the Lord empowered this weary couple to look forward to the coming DTS.

Mid-March came. Sungeun, whom I met at church, asked me for a favor, "Heejin, I can't read my Bible, so I need reading glasses. Can I go to your friend who is an eye doctor?" So on my day off, I accompanied Sungeun to see my friend, an ophthalmologist. While she had her eye exam, I thought, *I'm not going to be able to see an eye doctor for a while.* So I had an eye exam too. But as she checked my eyes, my friend exclaimed, "Huh-What !! You need to go to the university hospital right now!" At this news, I was anxious to make a reservation at the university hospital where I had received my training.

A few days later, I went to the university hospital with my husband. The test showed that both retinas were falling - without warning and without any symptoms. If I had come a little later, I could have become blind or had significant loss of sight. The professor who was inspecting my eyes said nothing to me but instead gave an order to the residents behind me. They were surprised at the sudden instruction but quickly moved me to another room, where the professor attached both my retinas with an emergency laser operation. The professor spoke to me at the end of the operation. "I did everything I could. The retinas were weak, so the edges became like netting, but I attached everything." The surgery must have been strenuous because his forehead was still shining with sweat. Thankfully, because the issue was discovered so early, I did not require a full-body anesthesia.

Joshua led me out of the hospital because my eyes were tinged with pain. All of a sudden, the breakneck speed of all these events made my husband and me wonder whether we were in a dream. Then I realized why the Lord had urged us to "Go! Go fast." It was because of me. What if I had been so busy with work that I didn't know anything about the state of my eyes and had missed the timing for surgery? What if Sungeun hadn't told me she wanted reading glasses? What if I hadn't seen the doctor? What if my friend hadn't found the problem? What if the professor, an authority in the retinal field, was at an overseas conference? What ifs flooded my mind one after the other. This experience taught me that one of the reasons for obeying the word of the Lord is for my own sake. The Lord, who knows everything, hastened to protect me from tremendous danger. I realized that the words He said to me, "Go now. Go fast. Go quickly," were His special protection. I still shiver whenever I think about that time, and I am grateful for the Lord's protection of my sight.

CHAPTER 3

My little friend

There was a time when I wanted to really feel and know the love of the Lord, but I could not. There was a small friend I'm thankful to and that helped me feel God's love ... With small, round black eyes, a flat nose, soft light yellow hair, and four feet, that friend is a silky terrier named Mauru. How troublesome he was! The list of all his antics can quickly fill up five sheets of paper in 10-point font. Curious Mauru would leave through the door slightly opened and get lost in the neighborhood countless times. Mauru would secretly eat chicken bones, raw barley, and all manner of foods he shouldn't have eaten because he would get stomach problems.

Mauru also could not control his instincts, so he marked his territory anywhere - a couch, bed, or desk. He was a type of hunting dog, but whenever he saw a dog that was slightly bigger than he was, he would hide behind me. As a pet dog, Mauru was such a rascal. Nevertheless, he had something special that only my eyes could see. Perhaps all dog owners will understand. After getting in trouble and being scolded, Mauru would sneak behind the refrigerator or into the blanket and peek at me. I would warn him, "I can still see you!" Although I scolded Mauru because he shouldn't behave badly, in my heart, I didn't want to reprimand him. Could he have known the heart of his owner?

One day after living with Mauru, I thought, *When the Lord looks at me, will he do the same? Is this how the Lord loves me even if I can make mistakes and fail?* In this small way, despite my mistakes and weaknesses, I began to understand little by little the unconditional love of our beloved Lord. When Mauru was 6 years old, he went out of the house and got lost. After I dramatically found my lost dog, I prayed to the Lord. *God, please help Mauru die at home peacefully. And help me to say goodbye to him. Please help me to endure the sadness of farewell, and I thank you for this precious time with him.*

Three days after my husband received God's direction, I heard that my family dog Mauru was very sick. He had suddenly taken ill. And now Mauru was on his way to the E.R. I heard Mauru's whining over the phone because he was sick. I cried that night. The next day, as I was on the stairs going to the morning service, my heart hurt as if it was sprayed with red pepper powder. I burst out in lamentation. *God! Would anyone understand this feeling? Do you know my feelings?* And I felt His voice telling me, "I did when my Son was on the cross." I couldn't say anything...

My heart ached even for my dog, but how much more pain did our Heavenly Father feel? I felt differently about the part of the Bible that I had skimmed. Now I can guess at a little bit of the heartbreaking sacrifice of the Father, who gave up his only Son.

Three weeks later, on March 14, my brother contacted me saying, "Mauru is gone." The previous night, in my dream, Mauru was lying on my arm. I went to my parents' home with pain in my heart, and he was lying in the same way as I had dreamed. When I was tired and sad, he would come up to me and comfort me with his little body, and when I arrived home late at night when everyone was asleep, he would wake up and welcome me with sleepy eyes. I said goodbye to this small friend who loved me so sweetly.

Several weeks had passed since he left, but my heart was still heavy. Then I read a story in a devotional that I read during my QT. The passage was written by an auntie who accepted the Lord because of her niece Eunyung who went to heaven at a young age. As she prayed in her sorrow, she felt the voice of the Lord saying, *Eunkyung is in my arms. Eunkyung is my servant sent to lead you to salvation. You could be buried in the world and fall into eternal hell fire. So I tried to protect you through Eunkyung.* Upon seeing this article, the sorrow that filled my heart began to subside. And I was able to process my thoughts about what I felt and realized through Mauru.

And in response to those prayers from four years ago, I could now pray. "Lord, thank you for sending Mauru to this world. I miss him a lot, but I still want to thank you for the memories I had with him. And thank you for letting me know Your unconditional love." In this way, Mauru showed me the love of the Lord both when he was with me and when he left.

Fig 3. My little friend Mauru

CHAPTER 4

The Door Opens

My husband was able to finish his work commitments a month early and was taking care of our South African visas and our household items. When preparing for marriage, my husband had asked me to buy used things for us newlyweds. What a shock! My husband grew up in the United States, and he was a 1.5 generation Korean-American. And I am a Korean deep in my bones. Our cultural differences spanned the width of the Pacific!

On one of our dates, we met in front of the church, and Joshua gave me a banana and asked me which way I opened it. He was a fun and a bit of an eccentric boyfriend. While thinking, *"What is he talking about?,"* I peeled the banana by opening the end as usual. Then he was amazed and said that he peeled from the opposite side and broke the part connected to the stem. At the same time, he said with excitement that the US dials 911 for emergencies, but Korea calls 119. He went on to say that he knew that the way I did things was because I loved him in a Korean way. Back then, I didn't really understand, but later on, I saw he was trying to understand the cultural differences that existed between us.

During our newlywed life, my heart really didn't want used things. Nevertheless, I tried to follow my husband because he had good reasons. However, a desire for a new electric rice cooker and a new bed was simply impossible to give up. I couldn't get over it. It seems that the Lord understood my heart. I didn't tell anyone about these desires, but in addition to a new rice cooker, new household items thankfully came in through my family and friends. And my college friends bought me a new bed!! But in planning to travel abroad for at least four to five years, we could not take them with us. Regrettably, I had to sell almost everything I could. Each time I returned home from work, one or two items had disappeared. Then one day, my favorite item, the bed, was sold. When I saw the empty section of the room where the bed used to be, I felt empty. I still remember that scene... But at least I had been using a new bed for the last two years! I comforted myself with that thought. After the experiences of those days, and taking after my husband, I am also SSRR (saving, sharing, receiving, recycling). And so we entered the world of minimalism~

Soon after, our church's medical mission team, Dream Team, held a missions commissioning ceremony for us. The Dream Team members were surprised that Joshua and I quit our jobs to go to DTS, but they encouraged us by saying that we were brave. For us, the Dream Team was like a family. Thank you for blessing and loving us. I met the Dream Team for the first time during my second year as a resident. I read about a special service called Medical Night in Onnuri Church's newspaper, and I attended out of curiosity. When the service was almost over, someone spoke on short-term medical missions, and the church handed out applications. For a while, I hesitated filling out an application. Yet I was usually interested in medical volunteer service, so I decided to complete the form as if I were applying. On the application form, Southeast Asian countries were labeled with A, B, C, and D. D was Cambodia. I had no idea such a country existed. It was my first time hearing of Cambodia, but I was intrigued. I checked.

However, I didn't attend the short-term medical mission trip in Cambodia due to lack of time, and I wasn't interested in missionary work, yet. In addition, I didn't want to spend my whole break that was only a week long on outreach. Instead, I joined the Dream Team's local medical mission once a month at the Mission Center, which was established in the church to serve foreign workers. I didn't even know what a medical mission was, but I felt proud that I could help people in need.

Two years passed, and in my fourth year of residency, I was preparing for a specialist exam at the time. However, I had a hard time because I decided to give up my dream of becoming a professor in order to pay off my family's debt. And my beloved grandmother passed away a year before. I couldn't concentrate on studying for the professional exam. In the midst of these difficulties, I had no choice but to turn to God. And I made the big decision to go on Summer Outreach because I wanted to get closer to God.

That's how I went on my first outreach to Cambodia! My new mission life started there. We were working together, eating, and sleeping in the same building. I became excited to go to church and see my church family. From that point on, my life was divided into two parts: B.C. and AD. I was able to grow up healthy through my relationship with the Dream Team. Psalm 119:71 says, "It was good for me to be afflicted, so that I might learn your decrees." This Bible verse applies to me as well. I thank the Lord for calling me close.

It was now May 1. We had to leave our home because our

house was sold earlier than expected. But there was no place for us to go. *Where should we go?* I SOSed Sungeun, who was a great supporter of our marriage. Although we made a burdensome request, she welcomed us to her place. We cooked together, went to church, and walked along the Han River. So concluded our last three weeks in South Korea at her place. May 8 came along - Parents' Day. We had lunch with my parents and gifted them red carnations according to South Korean customs. After eating with my parents, my husband and I walked along the Han River. Our stroll was peaceful, and the Banpo Bridge rainbow fountain show was delightful. Thank you, God. After finalizing our packing, we put our luggage for South Africa in two boxes and shipped them through the post office. They would take two months to arrive. It was strange to think that in two months, we ourselves would be picked up in South Africa.

Things were going well, but we had one final hurdle. Our visas! It was eight days before our departure to South Africa, but no visas had been issued. In the past three months, our documents had been rejected four times. *There is not much time left. But this is our fifth time applying, and we need our visas now.* Our nervousness grew day by day. On May 12, my husband suddenly asked me to go to Jesus Abbey. He wanted to greet Father Jeremiah (the Anglican Church calls the pastor "father"), who had officiated our wedding. I had never been to Jesus Abbey, but Joshua persuaded me, assuring me that the trip would be good for us. "Okay. My heart is burning here anyway; let's go get some air!" We arrived in Taebaek on a train and spent the night in a jimjilbang - a 24-hour Korean sauna.

We arrived at Jesus Abbey by bus early the next

morning. Cute, small buildings of stone and wood blended in with the surrounding nature. Many prayers had been laid up, so my heart was at peace and calm joy sprung up. I thought, *It was good to listen to my husband.* That day Father Jeremiah greeted us warmly, and we had lunch together. Upon returning to the train station, we still didn't have our visas but neither would we obtain them through worrying. We had already come so far from Seoul, so we decided to see the East Sea. In the opposite direction, we took a train to Gangneung. The train meandered slowly between the winding mountains. We arrived at Jeongdongjin Station. It was a weekday, so there weren't many people. We made a spontaneous stop to rest in Jeongdongjin, the eastern part of South Korea, watched the sea, and explored a cute watch museum. We added one more night to our trip and stayed cool by the ocean for two nights. The remaining time until our departure for South Africa was now five days. However, our rest gave us more peace and calm. While we were on our train to Seoul, a text message came. "Who texted me?" I opened my phone. The South African embassy had approved our visas! Finally the door was opened. Praise the Lord! Even when we rested, the Lord was working faithfully. When I think about that time, I can be at peace as I remember the Lord will be working. Thank you, Lord.

After an early morning worship service, I met my friend Mijung at a coffee shop. Before I got married, we had been in a Bible study on biblical marriage. We had read books and prayed together, and each meeting had been fun and practical. When I went to early morning worship with Joshua during our dating years, we often met her at church. She used to introduce us to good programs and books. We were blessed as a couple through these recommendations: a manual called *Freedom Class* (Freedom resource manual, City Central Publishing) and *Make Peace with Your Past* by Tom Sledge. On our coffee date before we left for South Africa, she took something out of her bag. Mini Kanu packets (a Korean brand of instant coffee)! She had tightly packed them in a ziploc bag! "Mijung... what is this?" "Just take it. It will be very useful." "My bags are already about to burst." "I removed all the paper packaging to make more space."

Flawless Mijung!! She left me no choice, so I packed the coffee. In time, I would see that she was right. Soon after leaving South Korea, where americano flowed through the streets, Kanu became like liquid gold. Whenever I missed the coffee I had in South Korea, I frugally savored the Kanu packets one by one. I was busy preparing to leave, so I didn't even think about coffee. Yet through Mijung, the Lord prepared coffee, and it was even my favorite, americano! God cares about the details. Rich and thick coffee adds a pleasant aroma to life. Even if my surroundings change, my love for coffee does not. Just like the law of gravity, the law of the appetite does not change, either!

May 17. We finished packing up, strolled along the Han River in the evening, and read the last chapter of *Daring to Live on the Edge* before going to bed. Reading this book over the past two to three months calmed me of my financial anxieties and worries about the future. I realized the reason for these anxieties. I had experienced the scars of poverty as a child, and as anxiety inside me grew while we were preparing to leave, I was afraid to experience such want again. So I hesitated and disliked taking a step in faith in relying on the Lord for finances. And I realized I had an idol in my life. How much did I depend on myself as a doctor and on my job at the hospital? I took time to repent before the LORD of the idol of self-dependence. And I have strengthened my faith in the Lord. The title of the book *Daring to Live on the Edge* is really fitting. I'm thankful to Loren Cunningham for sharing his faith in the book.

The day before we left, Sungeun displayed her cooking skills by holding a farewell party at her home. Joshua and I feasted on grilled smoked duck with Sungeun and Casablanca. In the midst of the love from these precious ladies the Lord had blessed us with, Joshua and I had a happy evening. Yet despite the fun, my heart was sad because I wouldn't be able to see my dear friends for a while. The next morning, we worshiped at dawn, and after that, I met Sookhyun, one of the Dream Team dentists, by chance at the church cafe. Sookhyun often said good morning when we had a cup of coffee before going to work after dawn service. When she found out we were leaving that day, she asked me to wait a minute and ran out of the cafe, returning with a handful of cash from the ATM. She smiled and told us to spend it on the trip. I can still see the way she ran back to us with a blessing in her hand.

Later that day, my brother saw us off at the airport. I was entrusting my parents to my brother, and I was so sorry that I couldn't say a word. My younger brother probably had a lot of things he wanted to say, but he sent us off with the words, "Take care of yourself." I was deeply grateful to my younger brother. "Thank you, Daehui."

I met Casablanca at the airport, too. This sweet friend

had taken a break from work to see the DLS and her husband off (Dear Lovely Sister...that's me. She likes to shorten her words). We spent a couple of hours eating together until we had to check in at the airport. Because we were going to depart, our nerves were tense at first, but we soon settled due to love and care. On May 20, we stepped into an unknown future and world with Casablanca's warm smile behind us.

Fig 4. Our departure into the unknown, surrounded by the light of the Lord

CHAPTER 5

Go up to Bethel

Before I ever stepped foot in South Africa, I had a location I needed to visit. Bethel! As we were preparing to enter South Africa, God told us to go up to Bethel first. So we prayed, *Where is our Bethel?* There was a time where I had a special encounter with God. It was the second overseas mission of the Dream Team that I participated in. The ministry is located in Kampong Cham, a provincial town far from Cambodia's capital, Phnom Penh. Missionary Kim was serving there. If you follow the Mekong River for about two hours from Kampongcham riding a flat, long barrel boat with a flat roof, you'll come across a small village called Jihai. Jihai still had no bathroom facilities. We rode on top of the flat roof of the boat as we sailed back from Jihai after ministry. On the calm waters of the Mekong, the boat was gently cutting through the ripples.

During this season, I had been pondering for a while, "Is the Lord looking at me, an ant among so many other ants?" That day, I was also thinking the same thought on this return trip. Over the calm Mekong River, the red color of the setting sun followed the boat. Seeing this calm and beautiful scene, suddenly a thought came up, and I said to the friend next to me, "Eunchae, is the sun following you, too?" Responding to the abrupt question, she said, "Uh... yes..." *'I see!! Wow! Even the sun made by the Lord is looking at me one-on-one like this, so of course the Lord must be doing the same!!'* At that moment, I lifted my eyes to see a clear sky with only one only one oval cloud with the middle open, and the red sun was hanging in the middle of the cloud! An eye made of clouds with the sun as the pupil. That day in Cambodia, I realized for the first time in my life that the Lord was looking at me that way.

Cambodia is also a special place to Joshua and me as a couple. In July of 2008, Joshua visited South Korea with the plan to stay for two weeks. We met totally by chance at our friends' house. Joshua was Joseph's friend, and I was his wife's friend. Anyway, after spending some time in South Korea, he extended his visit, and he also decided to participate in the mid-August summer outreach. At the time, Hebron Hospital in Phnom Penh had five small bungalow buildings on a large, dusty plot of ground. There, a pediatrician and anesthesiologists were eagerly serving the sick. On the last day of outreach, overnight rains had flooded the area. Eventually, half of the hospital ground, even where the office was, was submerged in dirty water. Even in this situation, patients flocked to the hospital area because news of the medical treatment from the last two days had spread even to remote areas. Team members set up tents for medical treatment, prepared simple tables and chairs, and did their best to prepare, but everything took time. While waiting on the other teams, I wondered about the state of the flooded clinic. My curiosity rising, the muddy water from my knees to my thighs didn't faze me. While I was strolling in the water, someone was coming from behind. And I saw Joshua.

All of a sudden, I stumbled into a hole in the mud. My feet sank in, and I tripped for a moment. "Huh?!" Joshua grabbed my arm. My heart was pounding. "What are your hobbies?" he suddenly asked me. "Reading," I blurted out without thinking too much. It seemed like he smiled.

"Would you like to have coffee with me when we go back to Seoul?" "Okay."

It was the moment that Joshua saw me as a woman for the first time and we first became interested in each other. Even as I think about this instance again, the question, "What are your hobbies?" seems a bit odd, but I would come to find that he had asked an important question. His hobby was reading books, so he was looking for a woman who also liked books. Even when he fell in love, he didn't forget to think and ask this question. Yeah, my husband is more rational than me. I later heard that when he saw me walking through the muddy water, he saw a halo around me. He thought I was a low maintenance girl. *Really? Am I?* Perhaps many ladies will agree with me that we are each princesses in our own right. Eventually, he discovered that first impression was a mistake... But it's too late to turn back now. Thus, the second official couple at Hebron Hospital was formed

And a few years later, now on our way to South Africa, we arrived in Cambodia on May 20. Missionary Woojung Kim of Hebron Hospital was waiting in the sweltering Cambodian night air. Hebron Hospital, which started from five small bungalows, was now a large hospital. What's more, Mr. Kim had built the hospital during the 2009 economic recession. He had been thinking about the hospital's plans for the future. At that time, the Lord gave Mr. Kim the heart to continue building the hospital in faith. For this obedient missionary, finances and equipment came from many countries in various ways. The two missionaries were very pleased that the second

Hebron couple had arrived. I'm so thankful to them. By the way, you may be curious about the first Hebron couple. They are missionaries in charge of the Clinical Pathology Department at Hebron Hospital~

The next day, May 22, I shared my morning devotion with the missionaries before I started my day at 7:30 a.m. The sorrow of many farewells over the past few months suddenly came over me, and I shed tears. Both missionaries were very understanding, and I was able to calm down quickly. Mr. Kim shared his prayer request, informing us that the opening ceremony of the Children's Heart Center was approaching, and permission to establish a nursing college had been delayed. While working at the hospital in Cambodia, Mr. Kim, a pediatrician in Korea, was trying to find children suffering from heart disease and taking them to have surgery in Korea so that these children could start a new life.

At the end of May, Cambodia was unbearably hot. I thought I was familiar with the weather because I had gone on summer and winter outreaches to the country seven to eight times since 2005. August in Cambodia, when the summer outreaches take place, is the rainy season, and January and February are the cool, dry seasons. The country is hottest in April through June, and furthermore, the missionary said that this year was hotter than usual. The dorm had air conditioning. However, hot air came out instead, so turning on the AC was useless. It was better to cool off with water and use fans, but we had power outages. Fortunately, the hospital was fine because Mr. Kim had installed his own generator. I finally fell asleep in the heat. However, I woke up repeatedly and slept on and off for an hour at a time. The rooster next door played a part in my inability to sleep soundly. That rooster! Every day at 2 a.m., I heard, "Cockle doodle doo!" *Ugh, there goes my temper! Maybe the blazing heat was also keeping the obnoxious feathered creature awake...'* I glared at that insolent bird next door on my way to and from the hospital. While at Hebron Hospital, I worked in the Dermatology Department two days a week. For the rest of my time, I worked at the pharmacy organizing the dermatology medicine. Among the hospital's medical units, the only place they used air conditioning was the pharmacy. Out of Mr. Kim's kind consideration, he kept me cool from the heat.

Our first Sunday in Cambodia came around. We worshiped together at the Korean Church in Phnom Penh, where Mr. Kim attended. The Sunday message was from Genesis 49: 22-26. "Joseph is a fruitful vine, a fruitful vine near a spring, whose branches climb over a wall." These words sounded like the Lord's strong encouragement to me, who was tired of leaving, parting, and the heat. One day, Mr. Kim called my husband and me and took us for a drive. We arrived at a samgyetang (Korean chicken soup) restaurant! He wanted to encourage and show us support so that we would not get tired due to the extreme heat. I will never forget that mouth-watering chicken! I felt the affection of this missionary who cared very much for Joshua and me.

I also met the missionary couple Jongsik Kim and Chansik Kwon (In Korean culture, a married woman keeps her maiden name.) in Phnom Penh. I got to know the missionaries during a summer outreach with the Dream Team. In the rural village of Toussala in Cambodia, where people suffered from malnutrition, this couple taught the villagers how to farm mushrooms. As a result of their faithful care and service to those in the community who were suffering and in poverty, these missionaries established a church. The missionary couple also invited us to their home. They lived in a traditional Cambodian house, which had long holes in the middle of the bricks to prevent the walls of the house from getting hot. The high ceiling and a brick vent in the wall provided natural wind. The Cambodians' wisdom in architecture was remarkable. Missionary Chansik Kwon cooked up delicious, spicy Korean fish soup. We had a good time involving delicious food and sincere conversations with the couple.

We had our second Sunday service with Mr. Kim. The sermon text was Genesis 12:1-3, "Go from your country, your people, and your father's household to the land I will show you." The sermon remained in my mind after the service. In the evening, I discussed leaving Cambodia earlier than scheduled with my husband. We prayed to know the Lord's will, and we received our answer in 2 Timothy 4:9, "Do your best come to me quickly." My husband and I decided to leave a week earlier than we had planned.

June 7. I accomplished my goal of organizing the dermatological ointments in the pharmacy and filing them in the computer based on their use. I thanked the Lord for giving me strength to finish this project. And on June 8, Hebron Hospital held a ceremony for the opening of the heart center. I could see that one of the missionary's prayers had been answered. This big, official event welcomed major Cambodian officials and the South Korean ambassador to Cambodia. During his speech, the

Korean ambassador said, "We are also building nursing college on the third floor." Wow!! Though not yet seen with our eyes, I felt these words echoed the Lord's proclamation, spoken through the ambassador. I was convinced that one day the Lord would open a nursing college. And in 2019, five years later, the missionary's faith has become a reality!

June 13. During the Hebron Hospital Monday morning service, I saw the front page of the church bulletin contained a picture. In the painting, Jesus was standing on the edge of a cliff with His arms outstretched, and the words, "Freedom at the edge of the cliff," were spread across the page. I was amazed to see the change from, *"courage* at *the edge of the cliff"* to *"freedom"*. Then it was time to depart after the service. I greeted Junghee Park in the dormitory, and she slipped me an envelope. When I opened it, I saw a neat and pretty card and $200 hidden inside. A "thank you" donation from me to her would not have been enough for me to express my gratitude, but, what's more, I received one instead. I felt the missionaries' deep affection, and my heart was moved. We also greeted Mr. Kim, who was working outside. The missionary gave us meaningful advice, saying, "Go where they need you." We said goodbye to them and left for the airport.

Our next destination was Singapore and we were to move from there to Dubai and then to South Africa. But, at the airport in Phnom Penh, I lost my cell phone. As we arrived at the Singapore base, my husband left his laptop in a taxi. Losing these important communication tools one by one was embarrassing to say the least. But a few hours later, a friendly and honest taxi driver returned and gave us the laptop. How grateful we were! We left the Singapore Changi airport and arrived at Dubai, a transition point. After waiting overnight at Dubai airport, it was finally time. Onward to South Africa!

PART II. SOUTH AFRICA 1

From Dubai to Worcester,
South Africa

CHAPTER 6

First Steps in South Africa

June 13. We arrived in Cape Town, South Africa. When we applied for our South African visas, our applications were rejected four times, so I was nervous while going through immigration at the airport. Yet we went through immigration smoothly!! Hallelujah!! We arrived a week ahead of schedule, so we stayed in Cape Town while waiting for our DTS training to start. Two days later, we took a bus around the city. On my way along the coast, I saw the red and yellow dirt mountains that I had seen in my dreams in Korea. When I looked up a picture advertising South Africa, I saw that these mountains were called the Twelve Apostles Mountains. When we learned about these mountains, we said, "It must have been right to come to South Africa." Thank you, God!

Another two days later, on our way to the tourist information center, we saw an Asian lady cleaning the street with one of her employees. *An Asian! Is she Korean?* As I watched, she spoke Korean. I approached her with excitement and asked her if there was a Korean market nearby. She invited me into her shop for a cup of rooibos tea. We talked about this, that, and chatted about small things. She and her husband had immigrated from South Korea 24 years ago. She told me that she would give me Kimchi (Korean spicy pickled cabbage). "Woo hoo! Kimchi!!" As soon as I got the Kimchi and came back to the hotel, I tore the cabbage leaves all by hand and took a bite. After coming to South Africa, I had a cold, and my body was aching because I was weak and sick for a few days.

Yet one bite of kimchi cured all these symptoms. I experienced the homesickness that I only had read about in books!!

June 21. While watching the news on the internet, I found that a big fire was roaring through Indonesia. The forest fire was so big that it completely covered the whole area with smoke as far as Singapore, the neighboring country. A photo of Singaporeans wearing masks was up on the internet. If we had stayed on schedule, we would have been in the midst of the smoke in Singapore. I found out why the Lord told me to leave Cambodia one week ahead of the scheduled date. Then, I had been bummed to throw away a non-refundable ticket, but it was good that we did. I almost got into trouble. If not, I would have breathed in the smoke from the burning trees and would have been hospitalized for asthma attacks. Recognizing the hand of God who protected us from the great fire, we offered prayers of thanksgiving.

As planned, we finally entered the base on June 24. The staff came to pick us up at Cape Town and take us to the base which was a 2-hour drive away through the highlands. After traversing a long tunnel, past the plains with vineyards and fruit farms on both sides, we finally reached the Worcester Base. We registered at the office and arrived at our accommodation. There were dormitories for singles, couples, and families. At that time, the couple building was full, so we were assigned to a family dormitory, which had an empty room. Our room was past the long corridor on the second floor and at the end of the hall! We opened a large wooden door and entered. One bed, one wardrobe, and one small dining table took up the simple, rectangular room. I missed my bed in Korea.

I held back a sigh. "Ah! I'm tired~ I'll just wash my face!" I took my toiletries and went to the bathroom. But when I looked at the bathroom, community life became even more real before my eyes. My mind drew a blank. Everyone has one or two Achilles' heels. For me, my spot of weakness is the bathroom! Even if it were small, I wanted my own clean and private bathroom! *That space is very important, but what do I do?! I can't imagine having to share a bathroom with multiple people. Ah~!! Besides, if I want to go to the bathroom on a pitch-black night, I have to go through a long, dark hallway. I can't stand being alone in the dark ... OH NOOOO!!* I was scared of night falling. I determined not to drink water in the evening!!

I wrote about my woes in my diary that day. *Arrived at the Worcester Base. The people are kind and nice. But...I complained to my husband about the bathroom. He suggested as a solution that we go to the Rwanda base. He said that there's a private bathroom and a private space...* (Husbands! In this case, it is best to just listen.) *Rwanda?!! Where's that?! In the end, I had a fight with Joshua that evening because he suggested going to the Rwanda base. My heart is growing heavy.*

And the words that were remembered from QT that day are... *Deuteronomy 29 - The new covenant. Serve only God! Psalm 119:71 - It was good for me to be afflicted so that... Matthew 4 - Jesus was tempted and overcame temptation by the Word. But the words from QT don't help. I am angry at God for allowing me to be in a difficult situation.*

I couldn't sleep because it was rainy all night and my heart was distracted. I was finally able to sleep at 4:30 a.m. The whirlwind of a first day passed like this. The next day. Unlike the day before, I was comforted by God's words. My heart grew soft, and I wrote, *God comforts and encourages in the Word and reminds me of His constant promises.* That day, the Lord also comforted Joshua and me by showing us rainbows and through our beloved Sukyung who unexpectedly sent financial support. I was so comforted and strengthened that I could see Matthew 5:16. "In the same way, let your light shine before others, that they may see your good deeds and glorify your Father in heaven." I applied these words and decided to write my prayer letter. I prayed, *Please help me to write according to your Word: honestly and well without any hypocrisy or trying to appear better.*

◆ Letter to Dream team and Friends - June 28, 2013

Hello~How have you all been? By God's grace, my husband and I have arrived at the YWAM base in Worcester, South Africa. Worcester is a small town on the mountainside, an hour and a half away from the capital, Cape Town. In South Africa, we're in the middle of winter, the rainy season. The weather is so cold that I'm wearing padded vests with fleece lined pants. However, I'm glad to feel the coolness of South African weather because I suffered from the dry, hot weather in Cambodia. Korea is said to be very hot these days... Take care of your health and fightig-cheers!!

We left Incheon on May 20 and spent three weeks with missionaries at Hebron Hospital in Cambodia. It was a short time, but I could experience life on the mission field and see God, who worked through them. There, Joshua taught English to local staff and missionaries. I treated patients, worked in a pharmacy, and set up a system for prescribing dermatological ointments.

Looking at the missionaries, I asked myself, "What is the driving force behind the missionaries here? What is the secret of the missionaries' lives?" These questions reverberated in my mind. I hadn't answered them yet. But three weeks quickly passed, and it was time to say good-bye to the missionaries. We received a lot of love and consideration from the missionaries at Hebron Hospital including Woojeong Kim and Junghee Park, and Missionaries Jongsik Kim and Chansik Kwon sent from Onnuri Church. We left for Singapore saying goodbye to our missionaries, and we took our flight to South Africa from there.

There's a saying that tells us if we leave our country, we all become patriots, and I could feel the truth of these words a little bit. I dream of eating Korean food, and I'm always glad to see Asian people. Why am I craving Kimchi so much?! After a week, God, who knows our desire and needs, had us meet a Korean woman on the street by His grace. And she gave me kimchi. How delicious it was... Hallelujah just erupted from my lips.

I missed Korea so much, and I felt pressured to do DTS in an unfamiliar environment in South Africa. But today, on my way to the base office, there was a huge rainbow in the sky, perfectly shaped. Wow! In front of the beautiful rainbow, I remembered that God gives His Word of promise and fulfills it. He is the God of covenant and the God of comfort. The passage from the M'Cheyne Bible

Reading that day included Isaiah 57:15 - "I live in a high and holy place, but also with the one who is contrite and lowly in spirit, to revive the spirit of the lowly" - and Psalm 119:76 - "May your unfailing love be my comfort, according to your promise to your servant."

In the evening, happy encouragement from Korea came in an email. The Word, the Rainbow, and the Encouragement of Love... The hand of God's grace that knows and cares for us continues with us today. And through this experience, I was able to feel the answers to the questions I had in Cambodia. He answered me with His presence and comfort. Our bodies and minds are having trouble adapting to a strange and foreign land, but we are expecting much of God, who makes all things work together to expand our faith and understanding.

Our prayer topics are - For DTS training starting this Sunday, that I will know God more and feel His love. To be safe with God's protection while in South Africa. To adapt well to the community life. For our allergies and sinus problems. I want to see everyone. I pray that everyone will be healthy in the hot summer and overflow with grace and peace in the Lord.

Joshua and Heejin from South Africa~

CHAPTER 7

Starting Awakening DTS(ADTS)

June 30. Our first class started. The long classroom was full of people. Our school has seven staff members: Victor from Switzerland, Daniel, Aquila, and Matthew from South Africa, Paul from Nigeria, Brian from Zimbabwe, Carol from Finland, and Nathan from America. Victor was our base leader and the first ADTS leader. We also had 22 students - nine men and thirteen women of ages ranging from 17 to 69. The students were from South Africa, Brazil, Angola, France (originally from Madagascar), Ghana, and India, and there were four Americans, two Zimbabweans, and two Koreans. The base's support staff included Victor's wife Wendy, base staff member Joyce, Cindy from Brazil, and Daniel's wife Maria. People representing five continents and twelve countries were all gathered in one place. Wow~~!!

Our packed school schedule included: class from Monday to Friday, ministry serving the community once a week, and a weekly group meeting called one-on-one, in which one leader and three students share their DTS life, do homework, and grow in personal relationships. We also had Wednesday morning service and a Thursday evening service for all of the base staff and students. Then weekends were free time. Yeah!!! On Sunday, we worshiped at the local church we wanted to attend. Three different kinds of work duty took up the rest of the week. Students were divided into groups and did their assigned work from Monday to Friday. On weekends, we might have weekend meal duty, which consisted of making meals for the whole base, serving food, and cleaning the kitchen. Finally, the third duty involved cleaning up the public areas of our dormitory.

We opened with orientation, and the first week of class began. In the long, narrow classroom, the tables were arranged in a rectangular shape with one side open. Twenty-two students sat around the table, listening to the lecture. The first instructor passionately taught us. But I could not understand what he said. I came up against the barrier of English! And the clincher - he had a strong South African accent. *Is he speaking English? What is he saying?* I looked around, and it looked like all the other students were sitting quietly and listening to the lecture without any problems. *I'm the only one who can't keep up*, I guessed. *I should have studied English more*, I thought regretfully. The first three days went by. Later at lunch time, I overheard that Angel, who was American, couldn't understand the instructor's strong accent either, so she was just smiling in class. Thank God!! I wasn't the only one. I was a little comforted to hear that a native English speaker had the same difficulty.

One-on-ones. Joyce, one of the base leaders and an ADTS assistant staff, and three students, including me, were grouped together. At the first meeting, Joyce introduced one-on-ones, and she explained to us our homework that was due the next meeting. She asked us to use a variety of ways to freely express what impressed us during QT and lectures. To give us examples, Joyce showed us what she had written and drawn when she was a DTS student. She flipped through many drawings. I was in trouble. *Uh-oh! I'm not good at drawing*. It's a burden...The phrase Joyce used, "freely express yourself," was so difficult for me to hear. I had heard that one-on-ones were good, but they started to feel burdensome because of the homework. Thus, I said stubbornly that I wanted to do my QT style. Joyce looked thoughtful, and she soon gently encouraged me to try other ways. I returned with a heavy heart and grumbled to my husband. My husband's answer was to not comment. In times like this, no response is the wisest answer~~

The second one-on-one was approaching. NOoooo!!! It was time to do my homework! *When in Rome, do as the Romans do! Come on, Heejin! You've always been an obedient student!* I encouraged myself, but… still… *I don't want to do it.* But the thought, *You have to obey the leader,* came to mind. With a sigh, I thought, *Okay, let's just try. Freely express...She told me to try drawing. What do I draw? Oh! Let's draw the rainbow I saw the first day.* I slowly drew a tiny fingernail-sized arch with seven colors in one corner of the notebook. *Alright! Next, how about adding some wildflowers?* I went outside and picked two small yellow flowers and attached them with scotch tape. In this way, I finished my first homework. I felt much better.

Next was work duty. My work duty group had four members, including two Brazilian students from the ELS English class and Denise from South Africa, one of the ADTS students. After class, we ate lunch and began to work at 2 o'clock. We had a weekly rotation of assigned areas, which varied from washing the base's cars, cleaning each area of the base, and preparing food according to the meal plan (We called it veggie prep.). Some work duties ended early, but some of them took all afternoon.

Whenever I passed a team working almost till evening, I thought, *Poor guys*. But not too soon after, my team had to work long hours. Most students worked their tails off because we had more free time if we finished work duty early.

Though each student might have a different opinion, to me, among the work duties, the flower of our community life was cleaning the toilets! Out of all the toilet cleaning, number one was cleaning the bathroom of the family dormitory, which I had to do alone!! About five to six families stayed together on the second floor of the family dormitory building where we stayed, and the women and children shared one bathroom. Because this restroom was public, its cleanliness was essential! We took turns cleaning every day. On my first day of cleaning, I cleaned a toilet for the first time in 20 years - since high school! I followed the instructions and added green liquid detergent to the bucket and mixed it with water. Hmmm. Okay. I was off to a good start. I sprinkled the prepared detergent water on the floor. 'Let's make this floor clean!!'

Then I tried to wash the floor with water, but something was wrong. 'Ah!! Where is the drain on the floor?' Oops!!… The bathroom was different from a Korean one!! In South Korea, every bathroom is a wet bath, but here in South Africa, it is not. Here, you mix a small amount of detergent with water, soak the mop in the mixture, and wipe the floor. Then you wash the mop with water and wipe the floor again until the bubbles are gone! I didn't know that, so I mixed a huge amount of the detergent with the water. I sighed and started wiping the detergent with the mop. However, the more I wiped, the more bubbles formed. All afternoon, I washed the floor of the bathroom with a mop again and again. Fortunately, I finished before dinner, but the muscles all over my body were screaming. How much I hated cleaning the bathroom every few days. Even now, cleaning the bathroom is still not for me~

CHAPTER 8
Classes

In our first week of lectures, we learned about YWAM's basic values, such as knowing God and making God known. Edward's South African accent was difficult to understand, but I did my best to take notes during his lecture. At that time, I was listening to his lecture, but I thought 'What is he talking about??' Yet five years later, as I looked through my notes again, I realized he taught really important principles. It is right that 'the more I know, the more I see'. I'm glad I reviewed my notes. Thank you, Edward~

In the second week, two instructors, Mark and Jerry, lectured on Hearing God's Voice. We learned about the voice of God and about the work of prophecy. We practiced hearing God's voice a lot in class. One of the things I remember was "feeling heaven". We put our desks aside and stood in intervals and closed our eyes. With the instructor's guidance, we stepped forward as if we were entering the gates of heaven! If you ask me how it was?... It was just dark! There were shouts coming from here and there.... But I was just standing in the classroom with my eyes closed...

Even when I was in Korea, when pastors and elders prayed for each person during a special dawn prayer, the people who were in front of and behind me, even my brother who went with me, were lying down after receiving prayer, but I just stood straight, unaffected. "Holy Spirit, did you skip me?!!" I said inside my head... During the second week of lectures when we practiced a lot, I said to myself, *That's enough! No more practice~!!* Although I didn't like being unable to feel anything during practice time, the second week's lecture was still a useful time to learn many new things.

After the second week of classes was Sunday, July 14. We went to the United Church in the city center of Worcester on the recommendation of the base. It was a church with a long history in an old building. Then, it was time for the sermon. On that day, assistant pastor Mary preached. She had a gentle face and silvery hair. The text was Jeremiah 18:1-4 "But the pot he was shaping from the clay was marred in his hands; so the potter formed it into another pot, shaping it as seemed best to him." The pastor explained the words. "God, the potter, reuses us as clay and makes us new works. Sometimes things seem wrong and you feel strange, but believe that God, the potter, continues to work. God wants me to be a useful, good vessel. God is making me good in His eyes." The sermon touched me. *Okay! This whole process of doing a DTS will renew me.* When I imagined a wonderful piece of pottery that would be newly made in the hand of the Lord, hope arose in me, and my heart became light.

The third week. The instructor was Steve, who was the YWAM African Continental leader. He was a tall, bright, and friendly man. The subject that Steve taught was 'Holy Spirit'. During prayer time, Steve prophesied to each of the students. Then it was my turn. He spoke with a gentle but confident voice. "Now you are walking in muddy water, so it's difficult and sometimes you want to give up, but you don't. God is saying, 'Thank you because you didn't give up and kept going. I will take you out of the water and wash your feet.' Do not fear. For the next season, He says that He has prepared the shoes you need. You will be able to go out on the mountain wearing these shoes."

As I listened to Steve's prophecy, I cried. I was lying on the floor of the classroom (This time I fell down. Hahahaha! Hallelujah!), and I felt like I could see something. It was a scene of Jesus smiling brightly and lifting me, who was a little baby, high into the sky. I felt joy. In order not to forget that image, I drew a picture of it in my notebook later in my room. My husband said that he also saw something concerning me. He drew this scene of the LORD smiling and lifting me up high in the sky. In this image, I was the present-day me with a ponytail and was wearing rain boots.

My mom and aunts often told me about when I was a newborn baby. At that time, I slept during the day and woke up at night and cried. Even the man next door who was close to my family, shouted in anger when he woke up at midnight because of me. So my dad held me close, went outside, and circled a roundabout where there were no cars at night because we lived in the countryside. We went around turn after turn after turn, until finally, my dad cried because he was exhausted and frustrated. I'm sure they told me this story to say that my dad raised me the best he could because he loved me. Yet every time I heard it, I felt uncomfortable because I felt I was a burden to my father. My dad worked for many years in a construction field in the Middle East, in countries such as Kuwait and Saudi Arabia, to raise me and my younger brother. Dad went there when I was five and came back at thirteen, so I barely had any memories of him when I was a child. I knew these things and I thanked my dad very much for his love and sacrifice. However, a part of my heart held something like sadness because I thought I was a burden to my dad. As a result, I also thought I was a burden to the Lord. Even when I saw Bible verses that said that the Lord is pleased with me, these verses didn't seem to have anything to do with me. Yet after seeing the scene, I felt the Lord delighted in me so much. The baby was no longer a crying and heavy baby.

During Steve's class, there was practice in the afternoon. We were to listen to God's voice and give to the person that came to mind, what he needed. It was a very effective class because we could practice praying to the Lord, hearing His voice, and being obedient to Him all at once! After the morning class and work duty, we prayed at our dorm. The person who came to our mind was one of the staff. The gift was a watch. We searched our luggage and found a spare men's watch. Practice began. We sat in a circle and practiced under Steve's guidance. Each person at their turn called one of the people forward, gave the gift, and briefly shared. Both the recipient and the giver rejoiced, were amazed, and felt the gentle movement of the Holy Spirit.

Now it was Hanna's turn. She came forward and approached me. 'Me?? What???' Hanna brought a chair and made me sit on it. I was embarrassed, but I sat down. Meanwhile, she brought something else. It was a bowl of water! Then she knelt in front of me to apologize. She said, "As a Japanese person, I apologize for the persecution of Korean Christians." She washed my feet while weeping. She was Japanese Brazilian. We had a class before when we gave a presentation about our lives. I had said that my great-grandfather had been in prison for a long time because he was a Christian and refused to worship the Japanese emperor during Japanese colonial times. She remembered my story. We sat on the floor and cried together. We hugged and wiped tears from each other. That day I felt that the old emotion of anger was washed away. Even now as I am writing this, I am still grateful for Hanna's sincere and courageous apology on that day. In the 1940s, Japan persecuted my family for not worshiping their king as a god. I forgave them a long time ago when I learned about forgiveness at church. Yet my wounded heart still felt anger when I watched news related to this part of our history. However, that day, Hanna washed away the old feelings of hatred. My heart officially felt peace toward Japan. Hanna, thank you!

The fourth week of class. It was much better than before, but English was still a high barrier. One day, while listening to English in class, I got tired and I became lost in thought. Then, 'The truth shall set you free' came to mind. I opened my Bible and looked for this phrase - John 8:31-32 "To the Jews who had believed him, Jesus said, 'If you hold to my teaching, you are really my disciples. Then you will know the truth, and the truth will set you free.'" These familiar verses came to me in a fresh new way. My mother's side was a fourth-generation Christian family. My great-grandmother dared to go to church; even though she was from a Confucianist family, her eldest brother cut off her pinky finger, but he couldn't stop her from going to church. My mom strictly trained me to keep the Sabbath-Sunday and tithe since my childhood. I tried to live according to the Word of God like these ancestors had done, but for some reason, I couldn't feel the Lord's love for me. I wanted to feel more of God's love and had a desire to know the Lord more, but strangely, I couldn't. Yet on that day when I read these verses, I felt that the Lord already knew me and accepted me as a disciple. I felt relief deep inside, and joy sprang up in my heart. I wept silently for a long time in a quiet classroom. No one interfered by asking, "Why are you crying?" The classroom was full of understanding and warmth.

One day when I was struggling to adjust to class and community life, Joshua suddenly said he had a toothache. I waited for his toothache to subside after he took painkillers I had prepared in Korea as emergency medicine, but his toothache got worse. Night was deepening, but my husband was still suffering from pain! *Oh no. This must have happened because he hadn't finished his dental treatment in Korea. Oh dear! I'll do everything I can!* I put down my pride as a doctor for a little while and searched for "folk medicine to reduce toothache". One of the solutions that came up was "biting down on roasted garlic with the sick tooth"! Oh! We had some garlic. I crept down to the kitchen in the middle of the night, turned on the stove, and fried some garlic in a pan. Joshua's pain subsided a little after he took a long bite of the roasted garlic.

Next up was coarse salt! It was a salty solution, but we decided to try it. After my husband bit down on the salt for a few minutes with his sore tooth, his toothache began to get better. *'Maybe it's because of osmotic pressure... But why did the garlic work?'* I still don't know what the relationship is between a toothache and roasted garlic. That night went by ... and the next morning, we experienced grace. The amalgam that had been put on the tooth just fell off! The pressure on the nerves had disappeared, and the toothache was gone. My husband understood why toothaches are the most painful of all pains. My poor husband! His toothache must have hurt a lot!! We talked to the staff, and they gave us the contact information of a good dentist in the Worcester area.

◆ Letter to Dream team and Friends - August 3, 2013

How have you been? We have been in training for the last five weeks. It's an enjoyable Friday afternoon here. Lectures and worship services are over for this week, and I finished my book report which was due today. Now I'm enjoying freedom, hahaha.

Last week I learned about Missions & Evangelism. The instructor was Timothy, the director of YWAM Nigeria. He was humble, filled with the Holy Spirit, and a missionary listening to God's voice in a very difficult place. I was very touched to hear about Timothy's ministry to bring Muslims back to Jesus despite the huge risk. The topic of Timothy's lecture was "Let's listen to God's voice and obey and jump into faith. Do not fear!! If you do this, you experience God's protection and blessing". When I listened to the lecture, I realized I was bound to many fears. During the time of confession and repentance, I confessed my fears, and the staff and class interceded for me. Other friends had their own fears, and they all prayed concerning these fears and cast out the spirits of fear in the Name of Jesus. Then I was surprised when Joshua suddenly got up and confessed his weakness and repented. As everyone interceded for him, I wept.

There are 22 people in my class, and about a third of them do DTS in faith. Among the DTS students, the youngest is 17-year-old Angel, and the oldest is a 69-year-old retired pastor named James. James had seven operations for colorectal cancer. Furthermore, in April of this year his only son, who had just become a lawyer, passed away. James said that he is enjoying Awakening DTS, that through the school his wounded heart is healing, and his faith is being renewed. Looking at these living testimonies of many YWAM people, Joshua and I are also training to hear God's voice, to move, and jump in faith.

I felt God's guidance in a fresh, new way every week, so I'm excited to see what happens next week. I think I did well to obey God's Word and come here. Even though things are difficult, the grace that surpasses my circumstances is overflowing. A variety of speakers come from all over Europe, Africa, and the United States, and each one has his own English accent. Even though I just sat there without understanding what they said, verses from the Word came to mind, and I cried because I felt God's love and encouragement more deeply. Even if I didn't understand English well, I was receiving grace anyway which was such a blessing.

I heard that Dream Team has only one week of outreach left! We will also intercede for you guys from South Africa. Joshua wants to see everyone, and I also miss you all. We will pray that you will be filled with the Holy Spirit, spread God's love abundantly to the land of the Philippines, and come back safe and healthy.

Joshua and Heejin in South Africa~

CHAPTER 9

Adapting

As time went by, we adjusted to life on the base, and we gradually became more relaxed. I was also able to make cooked rice using the hiking pots we had. When I first cooked with these pots, I made a "three-story cooked rice" which I had only heard about. The top is almost raw; the middle is cooked, and the bottom is burnt. Joshua and I shared the middle part, but we were still hungry.

Worcester had only one shopping mall, and every Saturday morning, there was a small shuttle van that ran from the base to the mall every hour. The van was very popular among students who went to buy food and necessities! We also took a shuttle to the mall. Ah, the joy of shopping after a long time. How fun it was just to take a look around!! We bought fruits, bread, and my favorite - Biltong (In South Africa, beef jerky is called biltong). The beef jerky was not cheap compared to other South African items, but my husband allowed us to get it especially to encourage me~

There were about 10 families living in the family dormitory. A big kitchen was on the first floor, and it included three gas stoves. Meals were served to the whole base during the week, but there were many times when I cooked food for Joshua and myself. There was no problem when any of us cooked our own food because we were all considerate of each other. These dishes were simple and tasty home-made foods. I saw an African food called yam that was like Korean cooked rice and a Brazilian fish dish. It was fun to see the variety of foods! Among them, there was one dish that Joshua and I (well, it was really just me) especially liked. It was a triangle-shaped Nigerian snack that was similar to a Korean fried dumpling. As I passed by the kitchen, I was curious to see what she made. I asked her how she made this snack, and she explained. You put the seasoned vegetables inside, fold the long sheet made of flour into a triangle shape, and fry it. The crunchiness was perfect to my taste! Just thinking about it makes my mouth water~

Although there were a variety of foods, the cooks had one thing in common. Their kitchen utensils were so simple that it made one wonder if it was possible to cook with just these basic items. Joshua and I were likewise in the simplicity of our cooking supplies. We had a set of hiking pots, a small fruit knife, and a water filter that we bought in South Africa. What were the bathroom items like? They were more simple. The small, white, square bucket which used to be an ice cream case was my face washing bucket. We also had two toothbrushes, soap, and a towel. These were all we had. It was a simple living that I never imagined in Korea. But strangely enough, living this way wasn't too uncomfortable. Before we knew it, the simple life was becoming our lifestyle!!

However, I had a problem. I was worried about work duty. I couldn't wash cars and clean because I was allergic to house dust mites and chemicals. I talked to Joyce during my one-on-one time. Thankfully, Joyce took immediate action, and the staff members in charge considerately adjusted our team work duty so that I were assigned to veggie prep. I chopped up the vegetables and other foods. On one side of the large kitchen there was a list of foods to prepare for cooking and which shapes these vegetables had to be cut into. The veggie prep team's mission was to wash potatoes, carrots, onions, bell peppers, and more. Then we chopped up, grated, minced, and ground the vegetables as written on the order sheet. Afterwards, we cleaned up. Surprisingly, this work-duty was fun! I would be curious about what I was going to do that day and even looked forward to it. Our team members helped each other and worked with fantastic teamwork. But a few weeks later, one of our members developed an allergy to onions, and he could not stop shedding tears (more than was natural). Unfortunately, everyone except for me was eventually assigned to another work duty. It was really fun to work with them, and doing veggie prep together is a pleasant memory.

Let's talk about the kitchen a little more. On the weekends, there was kitchen work duty. Weekend kitchen duty required more work than on the weekdays, so the work was a little bit harder. However, it was a fun opportunity to make western food. The food I remember was lasagna!! I had only sometimes tasted this dish when I went to an Italian restaurant in South Korea, and I got to make lasagna for the first time during DTS. We put various vegetables and minced meat in a large pot and stir-fried these ingredients to make the filling. It took quite a bit of strength to stir the vegetables and meat so they wouldn't burn. Next, we laid out the lasagna, spread on the filling, applied tomato paste, and spread a lot of shredded mozzarella cheese. We then put the lasagna in the preheated oven and waited for it to bake. Tada~~Delicious yummy lasagna with chewy cheese!! After cutting the food into serving sizes, we handed them out one by one to the base students and staff who held out their plates in expectation of a delicious dinner. It was very joyful to make a meal and give it to them. Praise the Lord~

Although I don't remember exactly when this happened, one afternoon, while the lecture was in progress, two verses from that morning's Quiet Time caught my eye. They were 1 Peter 3:5-6. "For this is the way the holy women of the past who put their hope in God used to adorn themselves. They submitted themselves to their own husbands, like Sarah, who obeyed Abraham and called him her lord. You are her daughters if you do what is right and do not give way to fear." This verse was about Sarah's daughters. Sarah was obedient to her husband because she had a fear of the Lord. These verses came to me during my Quiet Time. I hadn't noticed these words until then. But since that day, this passage has remained in my mind and has been important to me even until now.

"Honey ~ Let's move out of Ur of the Chaldeans." "Where?" "Well, to the land of Canaan." "What?! Where is that?" "I don't know yet..." "Okay. Why do we go?" "Well, God said to me He will bless us when we go to Canaan." "..."

What was Sarah's heart like? It seemed that Sarah really loved Abraham because she followed him everywhere ... Then when did Sarah meet the Lord? Was it in a comfortable tent that her husband made? Hmm... I don't think so. I think it might be when Abraham lied because he was afraid and caused Sarah to be alone twice. She couldn't talk to anyone, and there was no one around her to depend on. It must have been scary. Perhaps Sarah desperately called on the Lord. "Save me, Lord...I want to go to my husband." But on the other hand, she may have been angry at her husband Abraham. *"There's no one to trust!!"* Perhaps, through such a fearful and painful experience, she came to know the Lord more intimately.

Many unexpected things naturally take place in our lives. Whenever they happen, Joshua and I had to talk to each other and discuss what we would do. My husband is older than I am, so most of the time, he's willing to make concessions for me. By the way, his culture is so different from my Asian culture. It is very different! The more I live with him, the more I find out about cultural differences!! My husband is a "banana," a 1.5 generation Korean who grew up in the United States since he was nine. He is yellow on the outside, but he has a Western way of thinking and is culturally Western. Only his taste in food is a mixture of the East and the West~

Furthermore, because of my husband's adventurous tendency, there were times when I had to face my fear and I made tough decisions to follow. But what if this decision was not what I wanted or something I had never thought about? What was I supposed to do when this happened!! By the time we got out of our honeymoon period, this problem was emphasized. *"Where will we go for outreach? What do we do when the ADTS is over?* ... There were many decisions we needed to make. As a result, we started off talking but ended up arguing more and more. Perhaps without these Bible verses, Mrs. "Smart" would have bothered her husband quite a bit. Besides, my husband already had a hard time because I was a "high-maintenance woman who needed careful care"...

I really did. Since leaving South Korea, I had become a woman who needed more and more attentive care. I had a lot of fear as I lived in a unfamiliar foreign country. Since I was afraid about the future, I often didn't agree with my adventurous and curious husband. But after I came to know these Bible verses, my attitude when I heard my husband's ideas started to change little by little. I remember the lectures about ministering as a family which I had heard at a seminar in Seoul for couples and during the ADTS. They said that the ways a husband and wife feel love are different. A husband feels loved by his wife when he is respected by her, and a wife feels loved by her husband when he gives her attention and cares for her. It's said that when this happens, their love tank is filled, and they feel happy. Yet what happens if I argue and disagree with my husband's opinion every time? But the real irony is that my heart wants my husband to look at and speak to me warmly, even after our fight... In times like those, I really didn't like myself.

A couple should look at each other and at the same time raise their eyes and look to God. This is called the wife, husband, and God triangle. The lecturers mentioned that in the strength that comes from receiving God's love, couples can forgive and tolerate their spouse and maintain their love for a long time. It is also said that a couple that only relies on each other will soon see their limit. During my sweet honeymoon stage, I couldn't understand what this meant, but now that I'm in my eleventh year of marriage...I agree!! This is a fallen world with so many difficulties that couples cannot resolve through their love alone. Like this world, my heart has nothing good to show. I realized that my love and my faith are too small for me to solely hold onto my husband's hand in this fearful world and walk while looking ahead without looking to the Lord. But I am so relieved that the Lord is still holding on to us. That must be why a cord of three strands is not quickly broken (Ecclesiastes 4:12).

CHAPTER 10

Times of Grace

The sixth week of lectures. Our instructor Esther briefly introduced herself and her husband. They had previously been base leaders at Lausanne, Switzerland, and they had obeyed God's voice to return to their native country of South Africa. Esther came back as an instructor and her husband returned as a doctor, which was his former job. Esther had prayed for us students at her home before the lecture, looking at our list of names. She typed the words from God on A4 sheets for each student, and she read these words out loud in front of each person during class, blessing the students and handing them their papers.

Then it was my turn. Esther stood in front of me. "I smell a sweet fragrance. The fragrance is you. You release a beautiful and special fragrance in the kingdom. I smell the fragrance of sacrifice. God says you have sacrificed much for Him, and it has released a sweet fragrance." Then she read 2 Corinthians 2:15. "For we are to God the pleasing aroma of Christ among those who are being saved and those who are perishing." She continued by encouraging me to pour out this fragrance and said, "The more time you spend in His presence, the more the fragrance of Christ will come out." Then she stopped talking and paused for a while before adding, "God will restore the things that small jackals have stolen from you, and He will bless you."

At her words, memories from my past in South Korea played in my head like a panorama. The Lord had kept me safe in every area of my life when I had trouble. I had no place to rest my heart, so I would run to the church and worship the Lord. I would pray when I was hurt and going through hardship. My life and the tears that I had cried were seen by the Lord. God told me through Esther that "the Lord knows," and this message was enough for me. However, she also mentioned that there is a future which the Lord will give me. I was strengthened because God spoke of restoration and blessing. Through Esther's prophecy that day, I was deeply comforted and encouraged by the Lord. The friends who had listened to these words laughed during our break time. They said, "You have a fragrance allergy, but you have a fragrance." That's right. It's the fragrance of the Lord and not perfume fragrance! In this way, the Lord wittily comforted me.

I also remember Esther's testimony of the Lord comforting her through a vision. While she was preparing for this lecture, there was one day when she was very tired. So although there was a lot of work to do, she played games on her computer all day. The next day, Esther was weighed down with such regret and guilt. She opened the door to the computer room, and there was someone in her seat. It was Jesus, and surprisingly, HE was playing a computer game. While Esther stood at the door in shock, HE looked back and said with a big smile, "Let's play together." *Wait a moment! The Lord was playing a computer game ... Moreover, I think she would have been thankful enough that Jesus forgave her for wasting her time playing games instead of working, but HE also said let's play games together??!!* How was I supposed to interpret this unthinkable testimony?!

It was hard to accept and was an unimaginable scene when I thought about the solemnity of the Lord. Let me explain. It was similar to the shock I felt when I saw, for the first time, a portrait of Jesus laughing out loud while I was in Korea. In the portraits I had seen since childhood, Jesus was contemplative as if he was a bit serious. It had taken a while to accept that Jesus laughed out loud, but He said that He wanted to play a computer game!!! But what was the Lord telling me through Esther?! I believe the Lord was saying that I should broaden my understanding about Him. And one more thing! The Lord understands and accepts our weaknesses, more than we can imagine! The Lord valued intimacy with Esther above all else. The Lord comforted Esther and also comforted me when I heard her testimony. I REALLY like playing and eating delicious foods. And I must have fun when I'm stressed out and eat something delicious. Oh dear! These characteristics were two of the reasons I didn't like myself. But through Esther's testimony, I learned that the Lord smiles at me and loves me for who I am. He is such a good Father.

August 12, the 7th week. Instead of lectures, we focused on reading God's Word. We read the Bible cover to cover from the Old Testament to the New Testament - a total of 66 books in just 4 days. Was this really possible?!! Wow!! All the ADTS staff and students read book by book. We read in the morning, in the sleepy afternoon after lunch, and in the evening after dinner, and until night. Once we started to read, we had no breaks except for going to the bathroom. Victor, our ADTS leader, encouraged us by saying, "There will be grace." Under Victor's guidance, we all read patiently.

A big box which Casablanca sent from South Korea arrived. Previously, she had emailed me, asking what my husband and I wanted. Joshua requested Gim (Korean dried seaweed), and I requested ramen. It was a surprise gift! Yay!! The box was packed with delicious food that we hadn't seen in a long time. Gim, Shin ramen (Korean spicy instant noodles), candy, cheese sausage..."Wow! They have this and this!" She had even sent a hotteok mix (Korean pancake filled with brown sugar and toasted peanuts). We gave the hotteok to the Korean family who lived in the same dormitory. I could see that the two young children would like it. There was also another answer to prayer. I had wanted to have an electronic English dictionary at that time. N sent me her electronic dictionary through Casablanca. She had said to Casablanca, "Maybe Heejin needs this." Hallelujah!! Due to Casablanca's gift, my stress went away. Although it wasn't dinner time, I went down to the kitchen and made dinner right away. I put a pickled sesame leaf on top of some cooked white rice and put the food in my mouth. *Oh! I missed this taste so much!! The taste of my home country*! God knew my weakness and encouraged me in this way. Thank You, God! Thank you, Casablanca!

The last day came for finishing our reading of the entire Bible, and we still had a long way to go before we finished. We speed up. The Worcester Base's bedtime was at 10 PM! The whole base became quiet, and the only place with the light on was our classroom. As the night deepened, we pushed ourselves toward the end. Finally, we arrived at Revelation chapter 22, and we read the passage all together. It was over!! Yeah!! Ha ha~~ Hurray!! We all forgot how tired we were and rejoiced at the feeling of accomplishment. But that wasn't all. I don't know exactly how to explain it, but as Victor had said, there really was grace. It's true~

During one of our lectures, we had individual prayer time. After the break, the instructor asked us to gather in the auditorium next to the classroom. He instructed us to walk around and pray freely. Students spread out all over the large auditorium. *What should I do? I don't know. I'll go to the window in the corner.* I looked out the window at the beautiful sunny sky. Then, something like the wind suddenly came to me from the sky outside the window. And I felt a small sweet whisper at the same time. "Because I love you, I brought you on this trip." I wondered, *"What can this be?"*, and tears also burst from my eyes. I heard the voice of God for the first time. Oh! God loves me!

I realized ADTS was the answer to a prayer I had prayed a few years ago. At that time, special evening lectures were being held for several weeks by the Church Medical Mission Team. The theme of the lectures was "The Cross and I". One day, I was very exhausted at work. But I knew I could receive the grace of God, so I attended the lecture after finishing work. During the individual prayer time, I prayed eagerly in the corner of the room. I said to God, "Lord, let me be free from this prison." When I was a resident of dermatology at the university hospital, my parents' business went bad, and my family got into huge debt. So, instead of going to the professor course, I got a job at a popular clinic where a senior colleague was working.

After giving up my dream of becoming a professor, I removed people's pimples and moles at my office. My patients haggled with me to lower the price of their treatments, and my boss regularly checked how much money I earned. My life passed frantically day after day in a small, windowless room. But the more distressing fact was that the debt wasn't paid off as quickly as I had expected. I felt this situation and my room had become like a prison. That is why whenever I was frustrated and tired, I used to look up at the ceiling and pray, "Lord, let me get out of here."

Several years later, the Lord faithfully answered my prayers from that time. I was looking at the blue sky of South Africa and hearing the voice of the Lord saying, "I love you!" Like Amanda Cook's lyrics in her song, "You Make Me Brave", His love crashed over me like a huge wave.

Fig 5. The Lord's love for me is like a huge wave

CHAPTER 11

Words of Encouragement

Meanwhile, I received messages from friends, my Dream Team colleagues, and my younger brother. These messages from those who know me very well, are short but gave me great strength.

- ### Hyunjeong (my college friend)

Oh my!! That was God's work when your schedule changed. Once again, God let you know HE is always with you. Why did you lose your phone again?! (She knew my history from when I was 21 years old.) I am very sorry that we couldn't celebrate your birthday because you left. Always be careful, and don't forget to take care of your health. As I pictured in my mind the ocean in South Africa which you had mentioned, I felt refreshed after being knocked down by Saturday's war-like work. You may not be able to contact me often, but keep in touch regularly~

- ### My little brother Daehui

Older Sister and Brother-in-law~How are you? Korea is so hot. I went on outreach to Cambodia last week. It was my first time in Southeast Asia and Cambodia. We had an evangelism rally. And on the road, we worshiped by singing and dancing. Lastly, we worshiped to celebrate the opening of the church (My younger brother is a member of the choir.).

I was surprised to see so many children at the church's dedication service. I think more than 400 kids came. They sat together for over two hours and watched the service with intense focus. They were cute, but I also felt sorry for them. There were praise sung by the choir, an instrumental worship, a song sung by a CCM singer, and a worship dance performance. We also gave out choco pies, towels, and more and then shared the gospel. I wished the seeds we sowed grew well there. I thought about how important your medical mission was. I arrived in South Korea yesterday morning and went to work today, but my body is saying that it's still tired.

Mom and Dad are both well. They often ask me if I got a message from you. How is life in South Africa? It's almost been two months since you left. Please send me news often. Take care.

My Dream Team colleagues went to the Philippines for their summer outreach. The news they shared with Joshua and me gave us the feeling that we were working together for the Lord's Kingdom. It's just like when geese fly in a flock, and they honk to encourage each other~

- **Casablanca**

Thank God that the package arrived safely! I hadn't heard from you even a long time after the package should have arrived, so I was really worried. My neighborhood mart was a little small, so I just put what I noticed into my cart without having many options. Then I went to a much bigger mart a few days later where there were many things that I had wanted to send. Pray and email me the next time if you need anything. If not, I will only send you gaudy stuff~

Thank you for letting me know how to read the Bible in a week. If I just go to the bathroom, eat, and read all day, I can read the Bible in a week. You could rest during your work-duty time, so that must have helped. Oh! Yesterday was my birthday! When I arrived home, your handwritten postcard had arrived!!! Even if I wanted to send mail so that it arrived on a certain day, I couldn't get it right. I'm happy and thankful; God loves me so much.

I was so happy on outreach; it was like spending hours in heaven. I felt peace, and it seemed like time passed differently on outreach. I served on the intercession team this time, but Deacon Sook actually did everything. I just took care of the visitors' babies - hugging them, helping them sleep, and playing with them while making eye contact. I was so happy doing my favorite thing. Oh~I still miss holding the babies in my arms.

On this outreach, God gave me His Word on the first day. It was 1 Corinthians 13:12. "For now we see only a reflection as in a mirror; then we shall see face to face. Now I know in part; then I shall know fully, even as I am fully known." Whenever the memories of those souls I met on the outreach fade, I wonder if it is helpful for them if we just come and go like this? But I realized that the seeds of the gospel we sowed during this outreach were not meaningless nor in vain. We can meet these brothers and sisters again in heaven with clear memories of each other. How great was the grace after having this revelation!! I was filled with a greater desire for outreach and evangelism, and I'm already happy that I decided to save money for the next outreach…

When do you go on your DTS outreach? Is your husband getting good dental care?

- **Team Leader Dr. Ju**

Hello, Heejin and Joshua~Thank you for your email. I can imagine you enduring in an unfamiliar and distant land as you rely on God. I am jealous of how you're trusting in God and living with joy in your new life. Indeed, I feel once again that everything we have is due to God's grace and love. Please take good care of your health, and I wish for both of you to be filled with the Holy Spirit while being in the grace of God.

- **Jiwon**

Hi, Heejin unni (it means older sister)~~ We finally went to the Philippines for summer outreach. Our team was smaller than before (only 32 people). We went to the slums, and it was the worst situation I've ever seen. I felt the same emotion that I felt during my first Cambodia outreach in the winter of 2008 (Our medical mission Dream Team had gone to Cambodia every summer and winter for many years).

Everyone in our team is still doing well where they are. There's not much big news, but we are seeking the Lord. It seems like Deacon Woo will be the next team leader. Mieun and Hyeon have adjusted to accounting and general affairs, respectively. Maybe we need to pick our team secretary soon. It's a big prayer request of mine. The position has to be handed over in God's will, not in my own way. But I can't make a decision because I don't know which of the two I should do - lay it down or continue (She was our team secretary at the time).

My family is the same; Dad and Mom are fine. Misun (She is my best friend since medical school). is still working hard and wrestling with her research paper. I feel sad about your absence and miss you. I saw your brother at church on the day I left for outreach to the Philippines. He told me he was going on outreach to Cambodia. I said, "Since we're not going to Cambodia, you're going," and he smiled~

Say hello to Joshua. Don't get sick [I get sick easily, so everyone worried about my health. I am thankful for those friends] If you need anything, please let me know. I'll send it to you. Since you're going to be praying a lot in South Africa, please pray for the Dream Team and for my family and me. Since I've written my first letter to you, I'll continue to send you news. I love you, and be healthy~

PART III. SOUTH AFRICA 2

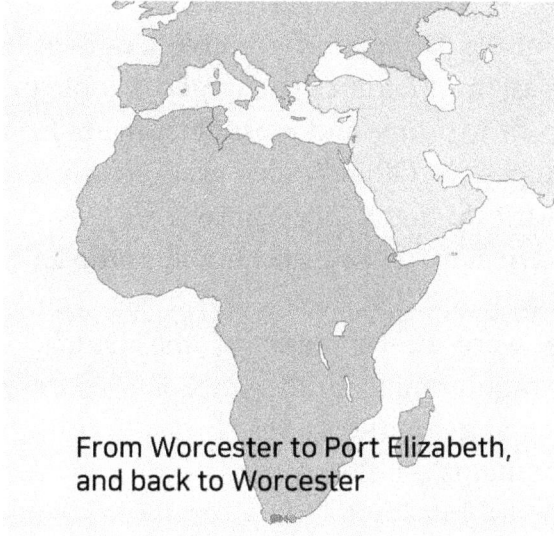

From Worcester to Port Elizabeth,
and back to Worcester

CHAPTER 12

People We Met in South Africa

I learned many things about South Africa after living there. Eleven major languages are spoken in South Africa, including Afrikaans, English, and Zulu. Afrikaans is a mixture of old Dutch and a native language. Also, South Africans are multiethnic. The largest people group are the Black South Africans, and most of them are from the Xhosa and Zulu people. Other people groups include the Colored (South Africans refer to the mixed race as Colored) who have brown skin, whites, and Indians who emigrated from India during the British colonial times. The White South Africans were descendants of the Dutch, British and German immigrants. South Africa is a country of diverse ethnicities and multi-cultures. It has beautiful blue skies, high mountains, endless plains, and seas. Various plants and animals live in the land and sea. Although South Africa had the pain of colonization and still had problems to overcome, it was a diverse and highly strong and tenacious country. It is a country where many people of the Lord remembered the great revival of the nineteenth century and hoped that such a revival would come again.

Then there is a really unique day. It is Braai Day. In South African 'Braai' means barbecue. In other words, this day is the day for all of South Africa to have barbecues. I don't know how Braai Day started, but it's a real national holiday!! On that day at the Worcester Base, family and friends gathered together and made a fire with dry vines for a Braai party, and the smoke from the barbecues rose here and there~ And there were memorable people we met in South Africa.

- **Anna**

Anna was a charming woman with soft and warm eyes. She came from a small coastal town known for sea fishing in South Africa called Steelbai. Anna was my classmate who sat on my right. On my left was my life mate Joshua~Anna was a friend who comforted me with a warm hug when I needed one. To me individually and to Joshua and me as a couple, she was a friend we were grateful for.

Anna's mother recently passed away. The more we got to know her and her circumstances, the more we were moved by her character. We wanted to encourage and bless Anna since she would have had a lot of stress from having taken responsibility for the housework and having cared for her mother. I had an idea. Since we had to visit the U.S. Embassy in Cape Town because Joshua's passport was going to expire, why not go with Anna? We prayed together to see what the Lord's will was. In response, my hands became warm. Many years ago, when I was going through a hard time, I prayed, "Lord, hold my hand." Then one day and afterwards, there were times when my hands became warm when I prayed or worshiped. When this happened, I felt relieved to feel the Lord holding my hands. So we asked Anna if she wanted to go with us. Anna asked us if she could. "Of course! Welcome!!" We got permission from the leader and rented a car from the base. We took a trip to and from Cape Town for a night and two days with Anna~

First, we took care of Joshua's passport. Then, following the navigator, we went to Cape Town along the coastal road. I guess it's not just Korean navigators that lead us by a strange route. Of all places, the navigator led us on a narrow path along a precipitous cliff. I was so scared that I couldn't look out the window to see the view. It was a road that if the wind blew, I felt that the car would fly off and dive into the sea. I repeatedly asked Joshua to drive slowly. There was a place to rest in the middle of the road, but I couldn't get out of the car, it was so close to the cliff. I felt I might fall off. It was a really beautiful sight. Yet I had a fear of heights, so I couldn't enjoy the view. However, I strongly recommend going there to people who are not affected by heights. But, for those who are similar to me, be careful when using the navigator on the way to Cape Town. The car slowly crawled, and it finally came down to sea level. There was a beach outside of beautiful Cape Town. We stopped by the rest area that was right in front of the beach, ate fried potatoes and drank soft drinks, and took pictures with Anna on the pier. I could leisurely look at the once scary coastal cliffs in the distance, hahaha! I also saw the seagulls and had an enjoyable time.

When we arrived at our destination, it was already evening. We stayed at a business hotel in downtown Cape Town. Because of our tight budget, we added an extra bed to a standard room (We had to ask Anna to excuse this in advance when we discussed the trip). The assigned room was at the end of the hall and had two windows. It was larger than we expected, so there was space despite the large extra bed. Thank you, Lord, for blessing our trip!! Joshua and I had the extra bed, and Anna had the original bed. The next morning, we ate a big breakfast and started our second day of sightseeing in Cape Town. We went to the aquarium inside the tourist complex, drove along the coastal road, and went to the habitat of the little African penguins. Oh! Small, wild, cute penguins!! They were swimming, walking, and sunbathing. Anyway, we had a good time during the trip. Anna was not very talkative or expressive, so we didn't know whether she had a pleasant time. Then later, I was unexpectedly thanked by Angela and other South African friends. They said, "Thank you for taking care of Anna," so Joshua and I realized that Anna was very happy. My heart was moved.

- **Tata James**

Tata means elder in South Africa. Tata and I had something in common. We liked Biltong (South African beef jerky). I sometimes ate Biltong to replenish my energy during our class break times. Tata often asked me to give him a Biltong when he saw me eating some. One day, I gave one of our staff green tea powder, when he caught a cold. He mixed the powder in water, drank the tea, and got better the next day, so he was happy about that. The staff asked me if I had some more. The amount that I had given him was enough to make twenty cups of tea! He mixed that amount in water and drank it all at once. Oh no~!! It must have been very bitter. Was he able to sleep that night? (Green tea also has a lot of caffeine.) Anyway, it was good that the anti-oxidants in the green tea helped him get better at once. Tata, who listened to that conversation, smiled and asked me for this green tea. I said that it was all I had so I didn't have any more. Then Tata gently thanked me with the same smile he had when he asked for some green tea and went back on his way. That day when I saw him, I had something to think about.

I often couldn't ask for what I wanted because I had a fear of being rejected, but I would later regret that I hadn't asked. Tata asked me for green tea with a good attitude, and he also had a good attitude when I had to say no. It was a fresh shock to me. How was he able to do that? His attitude challenged me. After that, I decided to imitate Tata and try responding like he did. "Thank you. Could you give me another one?" Normally, I couldn't say a word when I wanted to make these simple requests, so it was a big deal for me to ask. I practiced several times in my mind. After I had the courage and asked, I was so happy when I received what I asked for. Of course, there were times when my request was rejected. Even then, I tried saying thank you with a smile like Tata did. With practice, I was able to be more and more like Tata who didn't lose his smile when facing rejection. Sometimes, the person who refused my request was relieved after seeing my response. Rejection can be burdensome for those who say no, too.

Then, I thought of the prodigal son's older brother. I felt a little bit sorry for him every time I read it. He was angry and complained that he only worked like a servant. But if he had said to his father, "Father, I worked hard for you. Now I want to party with my friends, and I need a goat." Would his father have refused this request? Probably not. I think the father would have said to him, "You did a good job. Ok! Relieve your stress with your friends," and would have willingly given the older son a goat right away. I thought about what my attitude toward God was like. However, I found out that the way I viewed the Lord was a bit strange. Yes, I did. So I took courage and quietly requested to the Lord what I wanted like Tata had asked me. "God, I want to enjoy a cup of coffee." I couldn't believe I was praying for a cup of coffee. However, God answered that prayer. As I shared with the Lord, one by one, about what I wanted in my daily life, my prayer life changed. Over time, I was able to freely talk to God about the desires I had in my heart. As I did so, I felt the kindness of God, who cared even about my little desires. He answered, "Yes," even in response to my trivial prayers and to my small, unnecessary wants. As I experienced the Lord answering my prayers, praying felt more intimate. I grew closer to God because of Tata. Thank you, Tata~

- **Victor**

Victor was his Swiss name, and the name he received in South Africa was Luiso. Luiso is a Xhosa word meaning "victory". Victor was a good leader, and we had a lot to learn from him. He was reasonable, had a firm belief in the work of the Holy Spirit, and had a good character of respecting people without showing any prejudice. In accordance with his balanced principles of grace and truth, ministers and students from various places in Africa, Europe, South America, and South Korea lived freely and orderly at the Worcester Base.

Victor loved music, and he played the trumpet. He told us about his DTS story. He said, "One day I was very tired and angry, so I just walked along the river bank without any destination in mind. I poured out my bitter heart to the Lord." Yes, I agree. DTS is not easy. He said that the Lord met with him then. Victor also saw God's miraculous healing of patients when he played the trumpet in faith for their healing. On a special day when we prayed for healing during ADTS, Victor dressed up in a military band uniform, and he played his trumpet zealously. I was glad to see a good leader who had not lost his purity before the Lord despite his busy schedule and being a believer for many years. I still remember Victor who passionately played the trumpet.

• The Korean students

I cannot leave them out. There were Korean students in the English Learning School (ELS). Some of them were planning to do their DTS in South Africa, and others were waiting to go to a school in another country. Among them, three women walked around the Worcester Base every evening and interceded. Since they never told Joshua and me that they did this, we didn't know. But one day, we met them by chance while we were taking a walk after dinner. Three people were walking in a line and fervently praying in tongues. As we approached the women and asked what they were doing, they said they were praying for the Worcester Base. Nobody on the base had told them to do this, but they were voluntarily interceding every evening! Wow! They were doing such a wonderful job!

I felt proud of my country when I came to South Africa because of "Tongseongido" which means "praying in unison" but was called Korean Prayer! One day, a leader who led the intercession time during the basewide worship services said, "Let's do Korean Prayer together. Juyeo! Juyeo! Juyeo!" (This means "Lord! Lord! Lord!" in Korean.) I was surprised and amused at the sudden Korean words. I laughed and missed the beginning of the prayer.

Anyway, three Korean women intercession warriors! These were the faithful sisters who made me feel the pride of a nation that was famous in Christian history for praying. Thanks to these women's prayers I feel, the Worcester Base was more peaceful.

CHAPTER 13

Interesting Lectures

The first half of the 8th week. The lecture topic was "Destination"! The instructor was Ashley, the leader of a media school in South Africa. She was working to rescue women from human trafficking in Africa and Europe. As a Nigerian, she talked about her experiences in her native country. Ashley was tall and slim with a model-like figure. But in her native country Nigeria, this was a problem. She said slimness is ignored in Nigeria. In South Korea, many women try very hard to lose weight, so I didn't understand her story. Anyway, she was a woman, she was slim, and she had no money. She had all the three characteristics that were ignored in Nigeria. However, Ashley overcame all of this. It was a short three-day lecture, but she left a strong impression on me.

Ashley said that we are children of God and the light of the world. She counseled us to have intimate time with the Lord while being alone in prayer. She told us there are obstacles when we start what the Lord has shown us, but Ashley encouraged us to overcome them by focusing on the Lord, not on the difficulties. She also emphasized the importance of having cultural intelligence. She advised us to go beyond our own culture when dealing with other cultures and to use common sense. To do that, Ashley told us to study cultural differences. There was also something special about Ashley's lecture. She came to class with an intercessor named Phoebe. Phoebe didn't say a word. But the Lord knows best how hard she worked for Ashley and for us. Ashley and Phoebe - they were a great team!

The 2nd half of the 8th week. During the ninth lecture, Victor taught us about finance for two days. He informed us what a Christian's financial principles were. There are two systems of finance. One is God's Kingdom, and the other is the world's. In the Lord's Kingdom, the basic principle is to give and receive, and in the world, the principle is to buy and sell. Victor said that giving is not based on how and what I want to give but is based on obeying the Lord. I remembered what we had practiced during Steve's lecture when we had prayed to the Lord and exchanged what He told us to give.

The principle of faith continued to apply to finance. Victor told us about his shoes story that he had experienced. When he started his ministry, he had financial difficulties like many others in ministry. During the time God provided what Victor needed as He did in the story of Elijah and the Ravens. Victor prayed for shoes, and the Lord faithfully answered his prayer. Victor had new shoes! Yet it wasn't long before his gratitude turned into a complaint. The reason was that his wife was given a brand new pair of beautiful shoes. Victor complained to the Lord, "Why did you just give me casual shoes? But why did she get the brand new dress shoes?" Then he felt the Lord's response. "Your wife prayed to me for those shoes, but you didn't...." Since then, Victor's prayer life changed; he prays specifically for what he needs and what he wants like his wife~

How much money do we need? A reliable answer to this question is kindly explained in *Wealth, Riches and Money; God's Biblical Principles of Finance* (Craig Hill & Earl Pitts, published by YWAM). I had already read this book in South Korea several years before but applying it was a different matter. I started reading the book again. The contents struck me anew and shook my heart from the first page. "The New Testament actually contains 215 verses pertaining to faith, 218 verses pertaining to salvation, and 2,084 verses dealing with the stewardship of and accountability for money and finance" (p17). Wow, that's a lot! In Matthew 6:24, Jesus says, "No one can serve two masters; for either he will hate the one and love the other, or else he will be loyal to the one and despise the other. You cannot serve God and mammon (NKJV)." The more I read the book, the more I wanted to live by the Bible's principles of finance.

After Victor's lecture, Joshua and I decided to apply this book's contents to our lives. We needed to reduce impulsive spending and live on a budget! Changing our spending habits was not easy, and this was especially so for me because I had very little understanding of money. Joshua and I prayed to the Lord and budgeted together. I used to feel frustrated because I felt I was losing my freedom just by hearing about budgeting. But when I tried it, I realized more and more that budgeting wasn't that at all. Now, I think, "I wish I had started earlier." It's true~ But as the saying goes, starting is half the battle. I think it was a good idea to apply these Biblical financial principles even when we started late. Joshua and I are grateful to Victor and the authors of *Wealth, Riches and Money* for making the Lord's Kingdom come to our finances. And I am deeply grateful to the Lord for empowering us to put these principles into practice.

The 9th week. Ethan was our instructor, and the theme of his lectures was "Supernatural Life". He was the speaker who caused my heart to be disturbed the most during the 12-week lecture phase! As he shared what God had done in his life, many students were dubious about these unfamiliar stories which they had never heard before. One of the stories was about teleportation. At this important point in the story, I wondered, *Is this really true?!* I felt conflicted as if a stone had been thrown into a calm lake. So I decided to find out if the Bible contains teleportation or not. After the class, I looked for the Bible in my room. Oh! Oh!! It really happened to the prophet Ezekiel in the book of Ezekiel and to Philip the evangelist in Acts. When I found these instances in the Bible, I felt at ease again. We were surprised that teleportation not only happened during the time the Bible was written but was happening in the present day, too. As my doubts went away, I began to look forward to the next day's classes. But this time, jealousy arose while I was taking class. Ethan said he had been to heaven and had talked to Jesus. What??!!! I hadn't felt anything during the second week of class when students entered the door of heaven under the guidance of the lecturer. So I complained to the Lord. *Why not me?* What I felt at that time was, "Don't ignore your gift. Diligently practice your gift." When I felt these words, my heart was at peace again.

The last day of class of Week 9. Ethan told us he was fasting for 40 days. All he had was two rooibos teas a day, yet he had a powerful voice and looked healthy. I was amazed! Ethan carefully explained impartation to us. And he started imparting to each student in our class. One by one, we went to the front of the class, and the staff were ready to catch us from behind when we fell. My husband said he could see the fireball in Ethan's hand. Receiving the gift was so intense that even the staff who held us from behind felt hot and stepped back as if they were being pushed back. Then it was my turn. I felt something pushing. Afterwards, whenever I would go deep in prayer, I would feel something like a hot fire on my back.

Ethan was someone who spoke calmly and slowly in a low voice. He also spoke in a straightforward manner and only talked about the main point. That is why my notes from his class were simple. But Ethan's simple explanations are powerful even now when I look at them again. He said that reading the Bible wholeheartedly and praying lead us to intimacy with God. Doing these two things sharpened our spiritual senses and gave us spiritual discernment. Ethan told us that God's DNA is already in us and that through intimacy with the Lord, through love, and especially through obedience, the Lord's DNA in us is activated. The reason we live supernatural lives is for the glory of the Lord. And He encouraged us to "know God's plan for yourself, walk with the Holy Spirit, and have total obedience!!" He really emphasized obedience. The 9th week of lectures! My mind had a lot of turbulence, but I think my view of faith widened just as much. Thank you, Ethan.

Shall We Dance?

One two three four
Oops! My steps are wrong!
But He says, "It's all right. Let's try again."

One two three four
Ah~! I don't know the next step
But He says, "Don't worry. I know."

One two three four
Hmm… My steps are not good
But He says, "Good job! Good job."

He grasps my hands gently
And He says, "Let's try again together."
One two three four, five six seven eight

CHAPTER 14

Knowing Myself

Week 10. This week's theme was the same as last week's - the Supernatural Life. The instructor's name was Philip. He had worked with Heidi Baker at an orphanage in Mozambique called Iris Ministry. He told us stories about the jungle. As he shared stories about monkeys and other creatures, he taught us spiritual principles. One story was about snakes! When a snake is hit with a stick, the creature straightens itself out so that its bones are correctly in place again. The story's main topic was 'stretching'. Believe it or not, it's a jungle story. Anyway, I guess our team needed to stretch since Philip emphasized this twice. I learned that we are made up of a spirit, soul, and body, so we need to take care of our body well because it is the vessel that holds the spirit and soul. When I came back to Korea, I remembered the snake story, we were doing stretching exercises!

One of the interesting things Philip taught was about the 5 kings who were defeated by Joshua when entering the Promised Land. Philip said that the spiritual meanings of the five kings were the spirit of injustice, the spirit of entertainment, the spirit of unbelief, the spirit of religion, and the spirit of poverty and disease. And we have the power to defeat them in the name of Jesus, just as Joshua had the power to kill these five kings. 1 John 5:4 says, "For everyone born of God overcomes the world. This is the victory that has overcome the world, even our faith." Philip said that, just as was mentioned in this verse, the way to defeat these five kings was through faith. He emphasized the faith that comes from a relationship with Jesus. After I listened to this lecture, I thought about what things were influencing my life. How I was influenced in big and small ways by so many things! Joshua and I decided to drive them out from our lives in the name of the Lord and prayed that the Lord would strengthen us.

In these last two weeks, we had learned about the supernatural life in the Holy Spirit. The two lecturers testified about how God was working through their lives and taught spiritual principles. I could see that the whole class paid close attention during the lectures. Every instructor we had so far emphasized having an intimate relationship with God. Philip even said, "Someone who professes faith without a relationship with God is like a shaman." I was really shocked to hear this!

During the two weeks of lectures, I naturally had the desire to get closer to God. Joshua was also very moved, and he felt that he lacked hunger for God. He told me he would be doing the Daniel fast for three days. I asked him what this was, and he explained that it was a fast similar to Daniel's. One would eat potatoes, vegetables, and fruits without eating meat and grains such as rice and bread. So I joined him, but I was hungry. From the very first day, I thought of McDonald's Fish Burger, Kentucky Fried Chicken, pizza, and similar foods which I usually didn't think about. I craved them, but on the other hand, I thought I'd been severely tied to food. Anyway, I realized that I satisfied myself with food instead of God. On the last day of the fast, we had a special dinner! One bell pepper, one blanched broccoli, half a cabbage, cherry tomatoes, one large, raw sweet potato, one boiled potato, half a papaya, a plum, and two passion fruits were on the menu. Was the meal delicious? Yes! But even so, I still wanted to eat meat with rice. And a cup of coffee, too (I had added coffee, which I so enjoyed, to the fast list). I was pleased when I, a food-lover, finished my first Daniel fast. And for spiritual training, Joshua and I decided that we would continue doing the Daniel fast for the first three days of each month. I wished I could lose some weight, but that could only be handled by exercise~

The last week of lectures. The theme was "Feeling God with our five senses"! The lecturers, who were from Denmark, had a strong artistic sense. They explained that because we were created in the image of God, we were made to create beauty. They also said, "Beauty rescues the world." Through beautiful things such as music, poetry, paintings, and so on, we can help humans, whom God created in His image, feel free and enriched; through this beauty, we can meet and feel God. The lecturer's teaching methods were also artistic and free. During one lecture, They had all the students close their eyes and open their mouths; then he and his wife put something in our mouths. They were a piece of fruit, a piece of cake, or other foods. They told us to taste them with our eyes closed. They also turned on a recorded sound and had us listen. I had wondered what the instructor was doing. I see that it was a time to thank and praise God, who gave us our senses to feel these things, with our five senses~

One day, we all gathered in the auditorium. I noticed that there were large tables that were piled with magazines and had some huge, white paper. The lecturer told us to take whatever magazines we wanted and to freely fill the white paper space with them. After we finished, we would each give a short presentation of our work. At first, I spent a long time thinking about what I should do. *Ok~Don't worry! Just do it. Find whatever comes to mind and place it on.* As I started, I had lots of creative ideas. I cut out these images: an eagle, a kid playing in the sand with her mom on the beach, a plane taking off, and so on. I freely placed these images here and there and drew a big rainbow. It seemed like the freedom of YWAM had permeated me the past few months. The rainbow that I drew this time was at least 30 times bigger than the timid one that I had drawn for my first one-on-one homework.

When I looked around, all the students were working excitedly. Finally, "I'm all done!" I went to the table next to mine to see what my husband had done. Wow! The various colors such as green, ivory, and mahogany went well together, and rectangular pictures of various sizes were arranged in a straight and orderly manner. I felt like I was looking at a well-edited interior magazine that looked neat and cool! I brought mine and compared it with my husband's. Round, oval, and rounded rectangle-shaped pictures were attached here and there in various sizes. In a word, I was free-spirited!!

My husband and I compared each other's work and were surprised about ourselves. We realized that we weren't who we thought we were. We thought that I was a regular and system-loving person, while Joshua was the free-loving one. But in fact we were the opposite. It was just a misunderstanding formed by our growing environment and education. We learned about ourselves for the first time when we were over 40 years old. The fact that we knew about who we are gave us true freedom in many aspects. We could understand ourselves and each other more. Then we could lower the stress about ourselves and accept ourselves more. Thank you, God and thank you, our artistic instructors.

In the past three months, the instructors had been from Africa, Europe, the United States, and New Zealand. The Oceania continent, which was missing from the staff and students, was accounted for by the instructors, so all five continents were gathered at our ADTS. God had brought us together from around the world, and we were able to spend time together to learn, share, and worship the Lord. It was a meaningful time for me to learn the principles of vivid testimony and faith from the instructors who worked hard in their fields.

Each had a different character and inclination, but all of the instructors had similarities. They were humble before the Lord and man. They valued their family and friends. Instead of dwelling on the things that have been done, they were eagerly living in the given present, expecting what the Lord would do through them in the future. All of the instructors had peace and freedom beyond their situations! Perhaps it was possible because of the intimacy with the Lord that they all had. I think that their peace and freedom naturally flowed from knowing who the Lord was and who he/she was. During the lecture, I was able to see good examples of those who went before us in the faith. I deeply thank all of the instructors for their hard work in teaching us.

CHAPTER 15

Outreach Preparation

There was an announcement about where we were to go on outreach. Victor wrote Europe, Mozambique, Victoria Falls, and South Africa on the board. He said, "After taking the time to pray and decide among the four teams, write down your names where you want to go." There was a thrill of anticipation and excitement among the students. Joshua and I took quite a while to decide. I wanted Europe, and my husband wanted Victoria Falls. It was a huge waterfall that stretched across Zimbabwe and Zambia in Africa, so it's understandable that my husband wanted to visit. Classmates found out that we wanted different places. One of them said, "Your husband and you are standing on different sides of the river." I think this friend's statement was right. Joshua and I didn't want to give way to each other over the outreach area like a tight tug of war. When we did QT, we saw lots were repeated in the Bible. Lots!! Both of us were moved by it and we decided to go to the place to be chosen by lot. And for fairness, we decided not to do it when the only two of us were there but to establish it by a witness. Now that I think about it, it was a little childish, but it was a serious problem at the time. During the break, we made a note that wrote down four places, and Anna mixed and held it in both hands~

Ready!! I picked one with my trembling hand, and opened. South Africa! Both of us said 'Oh no~!!' in our mind and we were speechless. Anna saw our face which expressed shock, and said, "One more time. But this is the last time." The attention of the friends who were around us was focused! Once again, ready!! *Oh~~~ I'm shaking.* I opened it. South Africa! Again!! Our friends laughed...

That was how my husband and I decided to go to South Africa. I quickly put our name on the board before we could change our minds. Only two of us had applied for South Africa at that time. Of course, Europe was the most crowded place.

It was time for a final decision. A lot of people who wanted to be on the European team had moved to the South African team. They did not make it on their first choice. The main reason was that outreach costs were not met. We were learning something at that time. Among the Lord's responses, one of them is, "No!" As mentioned before, many of the ADTS students started with no tuition fees. During the lecture course, their prayers were answered and the tuition was filled. In the days leading up to outreach, many students applied to Europe which they had always wanted to go with the wish that HE would provide as before. But half of them had their outreach expenses filled (YES) and half did not (NO). Students who met the cost for the outreach were excited to go to Europe. But others whose doors remained shut until the final day of the decision shook their heads from the disappointment and rejection that their prayer had not been answered. This situation was in the Lord's big picture, but I was sorry to see them from the side. On the first day of the group meeting for the outreach teams, we gathered in the auditorium next to the classroom. I felt the air was heavy because most of the members on the South African team were solemn. Victor slowly moved on to the team meeting.

The team worked together to raise the outreach fees. The Mozambique team held afternoon tea together. Only women could participate in this tea time. I remembered that the cost was 50 rands (about $3.50). Instructor Esther and her friends actively helped the Mozambique team. Pretty tableware was arranged well on the tables covered with white tablecloth. The nicely dressed Mozambique team members served tea and sweets with care and elegance. Esther prepared by carefully filling out a prophecy on A4 paper for each of us who attended and led the tea time. It was a delicious and enjoyable afternoon tea. And it was a good time to receive the encouragement and guidance of the Lord through Esther. Thank you to the Mozambique team and Esther for the special afternoon tea time!!

All students were divided into groups for outreach prep. Our team practiced drama and attended a church in Cape Town where one of our members shared his testimony, and so on for 2 weeks. I remember Peter's testimony. Peter grew up in a family that was extremely legalistic. He said he could not listen to music at home except praise songs. He had a severe case of adolescence, and was deeply into drugs before he was 25 years old. He entered into a terrible state where he tried to end his own life. He was able to join our ADTS with someone's help. I was surprised when I heard what had happened to this young man who had a charming smile. And I could understand why at the beginning, he just sat quietly in class. However, as the class continued week after week, Peter's eyes began to brighten, and he began to smile more and more. While we practiced for outreach, he participated passionately and suggested a theme for our skit: the harmful influence of TV. It was a short but important message. We also went to the church in Cape Town, and Peter testified there about his dark past and how he met the Lord. Alcoholism and drug addiction are serious social issues in South African society. I hope his courageous testimony gave people an opportunity to meet the Lord and change their lives by His power and grace.

◆ Letter to Dream team and Friends - September 10, 2013

Hello~It has been two months since the lectures started, and there are only two weeks left. After that, we have two months of outreach. Unexpectedly, we were led to South Africa!~ Among the 21 students in our class, seven will go to Switzerland, four will go to Mozambique, and the remaining ten students will go to South Africa. The plan to go to Victoria Falls was canceled. One of the three original Victoria Falls team members discerned God's voice and changed to South Africa. One changed to the Europe team because a believer heard the voice of God saying, "Send this man to Europe," and paid for his outreach expenses. The last one came to the South Africa team because his outreach fee wasn't filled.

Hanna, the Brazilian student, only had enough money to stay for three months when she arrived, and she had been trusting God for eight months because God kept telling her to trust Him. And miraculously, her remaining lecture fees, her outreach fees, and even allowance to use in Switzerland were provided, so she will go to Europe. In addition, about half of the seven people on the Swiss team didn't have their outreach fees at first. Yet they were filled, so they will go to Europe, too.

For the last time we went for a half-day to a township where poor people near Worcester lived. I was really surprised because there's a huge gap between the rich and the poor. The weather of South Africa was quite cold in winter, so even though I wore a parka, I felt cold sometimes. But they lived in a tin-roofed house and there's holes in the tin roof. When it was raining, it leaked inside the house. When I saw the kids standing in the long line to get food during our ministry, I didn't know what to say. Anyway, I think there's a lot of work to do in South Africa.

I need to study English harder, so I can communicate more about Jesus in the outreach. I regretted that I hadn't studied English harder in Korea. But be bold with faith!! Let's go!! Yesterday I prayed that I would speak English well. Joshua's dental treatment was done, after root canal treatment and putting in artificial teeth. Thank you for your prayers.

For outreach exercises this week, our team will lead a full worship service at a church in Cape Town. Pray that we would be a blessing as the light of the Lord for those we meet during outreach, and please pray that God would bless Joshua and me to bear the fruit of the Holy Spirit. Hoping you stay healthy and victorious in the Lord!!

Shalom~

CHAPTER 16

Outreach at Port Elizabeth

The first outreach location was Port Elizabeth. It took 10 hours by bus from Worcester in the south to Port Elizabeth in the mid east of South Africa. After the bus started the crew gave the passengers a welcome box with 5-6 kinds of snacks. I felt like I was on a plane. Our team was pleased with the snacks. Delicious food made us happy. Port Elizabeth is one of South Africa's industrial cities. It is a port city with automakers Volkswagen and chemical factories. There, Linden and Jean were sent out from the Worcester Base and pioneered the Port Elizabeth base. Under the guidance of the new directors, our team served the region by traveling around Port Elizabeth for one month. The GAP church welcomed our team. The pastor was Rory Spence from Zimbabwe.

We started our first ministry at Ubomobucha on the day after we arrived in Port Elizabeth. Ubomobucha was like a daycare center for children. There we taught children, played with them, made lunch with the center staff, and cultivated crops in the garden behind the center. Our team went there many times! My favorite part of this place was planting! Watching various plants, pulling grass, and watering were fun to me. In my country, spinach is small, but in South Africa, it is big, giant spinach~ When we were planting the garden, the elementary school children who were beyond the fence of the building looked at Joshua and me in wonder. Perhaps the children had never seen an Oriental Asian before because Oriental Asians are rare in the area.

At the end of the day, team members gathered to talk about the day's ministry and planned the next ministry under the guidance of the leaders. Our team would gather at a YWAMer's house in Port Elizabeth. She readily provided our team with a renovated warehouse. We took turns cooking dinner there. We had some wonderful chefs on the South African team. Anna, Angela, and Jenna who was Indian-South African were all excellent cooks. Thanks to them, we were able to eat good food even when we were on outreach.

Our team worshiped at GAP church on Sunday. It was a good church where the Word was alive and the church was passionate about Missions. On the side of the church bulletin, it said, "We welcome YWAM." And it was written that there would be a welcome, introduction, and sharing by us at 9:30 AM. I was happy with the greeting of the church to welcome our team. The senior pastor gave our team members time to share our testimonies in turn for 3-5 minutes every week. The time came for me to testify. I was nervous to share my testimony in English in front of hundreds of church members who had gathered in a big sanctuary. I took a deep breath and read the prepared notes. I had misunderstood God as being judgmental and condemning. But even when I couldn't forgive myself, HE was still a God of everlasting love and grace, who loves me. I could finish well by the grace of the Lord. And my husband also shared his story. The story was about the relationship between father and son and God helping to heal it. Later, the senior pastor invited our team to his house. He told us his wife was a YWAMer who did DTS. We had a good time with the pastor's family, eating the meat that the pastor barbecued, and the food that his wife had prepared carefully.

Our team helped the associate pastor of GAP church once every week. He was a young pastor from Malawi. He invited the homeless to the church to treat them to lunch, preach a message, and encourage them. 7-10 homeless people came each week. Our team had a meal together, had a short drama (skit), and prayed for them. In the first week there was a young woman dressed in yellow who looked very sick. Angela and I prayed together for her healing. She had difficulty breathing due to AIDS and complications from tuberculosis. When we met again a week later, she looked healthier than before, she had brightened and smiled a lot more. Hallelujah!! Angela was a woman who had fled from an abusive husband and lived in a women's shelter. She accepted the Lord there, took the DTS course with us, and dreamed of working with divorced women in the future. We often prayed together during the outreach when we prayed for others.

Joshua and I stayed for two weeks in Jimmy and Eunice's home, one of the elder's homes of the GAP church. They had two sons, elementary school students, Matthew and Thomas, and two cute puppies, Jake and Buzz. It was a bright and lively family. And they had very unique pets. Eunice introduced them to us while she told about the happenings that the previous outreach team had experienced. One young woman from Australia, one day she ran out of the bathroom, screaming. The reason was...a small snake! Oldest son Matthew's pet!! It left its house and they couldn't find it for days. Then it was there that day. She was so surprised that she just burst out of the bathroom. Poor girl! Eunice just talked about what might happen to Joshua and me. *'Oh~~ no!!'* *'Which is better? To know or not to know that there are snakes in this house. The one I hate the most in the world is a snake! What if I meet them!!!'* Since that moment, every time I entered the bathroom, I looked at the floor carefully at the entrance, especially under the toilet!!

Thankfully, the days passed by without any trouble. And after a week, I got used to the home and was relieved. One morning, I was having breakfast in the kitchen, when Matthew came. He looked very happy. I said, "Good Morning~". Matthew proudly put something down on the table. I looked down and I could see a thin yellowish long thing on the white table next to my breakfast. And it moved. Oops!!! Matthew's favorite escape artist. It's the snake! *'Ohh~~!!* What should I do?' The spoon that I used to eat the cereal stopped in the air. My hair stood on end in horror. But I didn't want to hurt the child, so I pretended to be calm. The embarrassed child's mother began to tell Matthew to take the snake back. The child's expression suddenly darkened.

My head was in a tight bind. *'How can I face one of the fears that bound me which I had confessed and repented of during the fifth week of lecture! I have to put into practice what I've learned, but that's a snake! Lord! Give me courage!!'* Then while praying in my mind I slowly reached out my right hand, and slightly touched the yellow snake with a finger. I felt the cold and smooth skin of the snake. *'Uhhh~~~~~!!'* But I didn't take my hands off, and I saw Matthew and smiled a bit. Less than 10 seconds in total flowed in slow motion. Matthew's face brightened again. When his mother said, "Ok~ Take it home now," he was excited and ran out of the kitchen with his pet snake. Whew~~ I'm done, I was relieved. Then I met the eyes of the child's mother. They were saying "thank you and sorry". We encouraged each other with our eyes without saying a word. It was a warm morning. It was a warm, and victorious morning of overcoming fear and sharing love.

PE was an industrial complex. It was not easy for me, who had allergic asthma. One day I had to lay down. It was okay until the day before, but when I woke up the next morning, I had a fever and was not feeling well. My husband realized it would be difficult for me to take part in ministry, He told the leader who had come to pick us up. That day Joshua went alone, and I rested all day in the room. Eunice, who felt sorry for me, cared for me in many ways, so I was able to rest quietly all day long. Fortunately, by the time my husband came back, I had recovered a lot. I want to thank Eunice for taking care of me so I can rest well and get better.

Two weeks were already passing and our time in their home was coming to an end. They faithfully served the church and strangers like us. To Jimmy's family, the Lord encouraged them with Elijah's small palm cloud. Jimmy started fishing with friends on the weekends a few weeks back. But he had not caught fish yet. In the late afternoon of the second weekend, Jimmy smiled and showed us something. Two fish!! One for Jimmy and one for his younger son Thomas. Jimmy finally caught a fish. Yeah~~!! They were excited and had a barbecue right away. Eunice also had a good event. She was a lawyer, on the last day, she looked happy. She said that she will go on a business trip for three days. Lord, thank you very much!! The eldest son Matthew also appeared in a newspaper article covering the swimming program in school. On the first page of the newspaper, there was a big picture of Matthew with a big smile. His mother and Matthew were proud. I could feel that the Lord blessed the whole family with joy. As Matthew 10:42 says, He was the Lord who never forgets anyone who gives a bowl of cold water to one of the little ones.

The next two weeks were spent at Chris and Halley's home. They had a six-year-old son Nick, a four-year-old adorable daughter Romi, and a sweet black cat named Shaka who welcomed people. Romi came into our room, which was next to her room, and used to dance in front of us saying, "Do it like me." If Halley thought Romi was bothering us, Halley said to her, "Let's go to your room." Halley explained to her daughter why she should not bother us. As we gathered early in the morning and left for the ministry place, we usually had a simple breakfast at the kitchen table. One day we were having breakfast and Halley was by our side. Then there was some movement under the table. Looking down, Romi was wriggling on the kitchen floor with a blanket wrapped around her body. She must have seen a caterpillar crawling somewhere. Even now, when I recall that, a laugh comes out by itself. She was very cute and beautiful. Halley regarded this situation and said, "Romi, Let's go to the room with Mom." Then the wiggling caterpillar sprang up. The mother and daughter held hands and quietly climbed the stairs to the second floor, and we started eating breakfast. When they almost reached the second floor, Romi's innocent voice was heard. "Mom~~ Why should I go to the room?"!!!

Halley and Chris were interested in other cultures. We

wanted to thank the couple, so we decided to make some food and have a meal together. When we asked how Korean spicy fish soup was for dinner. Halley's beautiful eyes sparkled with joy. Chris, who wanted to please his wife, went to the harbor and bought some fresh fish. The big fish arrived! I first laid sliced radishes in a large long pot, put the trimmed white flesh fish, then put chopped onions on top of it, flavored it with Korean chili pepper powder, and boiled them carefully. I prayed, "Lord~ Please help it to be delicious." I scooped up the soup and tasted it.

Well, it tasted like something was missing. What more should I add? I was embarrassed. I asked my husband to taste it. Joshua, who was next to me, also tasted it. *Will it taste good??* He said it's okay. My husband reassured me that it was like a Thai fish soup. *Perhaps it's okay for foreigners to taste...Let's cheer up!!!* I added some more seasoning. I also made the rice and cut the crispy seaweed that Casablanca had sent me from South Korea. Rice, seaweed, fish soup, and fruit for dessert. This simple dinner table was set up. Chris and Halley sat at the table with their faces looking forward. Their eyes were full of curiosity. They tasted a bite with a spoon and smiled brightly. 'Hallelujah~yeah!! The couple enjoyed tasting the unfamiliar oriental food. Halley looked at the seaweed and said, "How can people dry seaweed so thin in South Korea?" Thanks to Casablanca for sending the crispy seaweed!

During this time, we developed a warm friendship with Chris' family. Shaka the cat also liked to come and play in our room. The day before we left, Chris' family and Joshua and I took a walk in the neighborhood together. Nick, who liked to exercise, left the adults walking slowly behind, ran first, stopped when the main road came out, and waited for Mom and Dad. That walk with a friendly and happy family remains a pleasant memory. We prepared small toys for the two children with thanksgiving in our hearts. Halley called me secretly one late evening. And she smiled and showed me her son sleeping. Nick was sleeping holding the toy we gave him. We both giggled at each other. Chris and Halley served us warmly for two weeks. I was very grateful to Halley who thanked us although it was too small for their service. She blessed me with a prayer for a baby and gave me a small book as a gift that she read when she had her baby. I was so thankful. That book is still on my bookshelf.

We served the places where Linden and Jean led us. Ubomobucha, GAP church, Port Elizabeth Salvation Army etc... Besides that, we helped local churches in PE. We met with local church teenagers, cleaned up waste and scraped old paint from the walls of the buildings planned for the local church center, cleaned up the garbage which was disposed of in an area the size of a soccer field in front of the village to support evangelism, and visited them with the local church. As we wandered around a large area like this, a month passed by quickly.

And now, several years later, a YWAM PE base is established in Port Elizabeth where our team used to go and serve. During the 5th week of lectures, Timothy, the Nigerian YWAM director, taught about missions and evangelism. 'Listen to God's voice, obey, and jump in faith. Don't be afraid! When you do that, God will protect and bless you.' Like this teaching, Linden and his wife, Jean, obeyed the Lord's voice and came from the Worcester Base to PE. There was nothing at that time. As they jumped in faith and faced the various fears they had encountered over the years, God protected and blessed the couple. The vision they shared with our team has now become a reality as a base for DTS and BCC (Bible Core Course) schools. Hebrews 11:1 says, "Now faith is confidence in what we hope for and assurance about what we do not see."

CHAPTER 17

Back to Worcester

During the second month, our team started our second ministry back in Worcester. At Worcester, another leader who had done ministry in the area for a long time led our team. We visited vineyards, fruit farms, rehabilitation centers in the Worcester district prisons, slums, elementary, middle, and high schools. We went there to educate, comfort, encourage, and preach the gospel.

I remember the owners of a fruit farm in Worcester invited us to lead a worship service. It was an apricot farm run by a faithful Christian owner. There were quite a lot of people working on the farm. We praised God together, and several of our team shared about God's work in their lives. Then we had time to pray with those who wanted to pray and bless one another. After a passionate service, we went out and found a large pot full of food. It was an apricot porridge with dried apricots made by the owner's family. Everyone ate one full bowl. I could feel the warm heart of the owner, and he hoped every one of the workers would accept Jesus and be closer to the Lord. In the return car, I saw our team members were holding a huge plastic bag full of dried apricots which the owner gave us to eat. Joshua and I also took some and ate deliciously that evening.

We stayed at the base in Worcester, so the accommodation was comfortable. But it was hard to travel around. Because of the tight budget, our team couldn't rent a base car. So when we went to a distant place, we all rode in a car that the leader would borrow. When it took time to get a car, we had to wait for him and car to appear. Then we got in all together in the same car, and went to the ministry place in a hurry. Our team walked around as much as possible when it was not too far away. It was winter, but it was not easy to walk around because of the strong sunlight in Africa. Fortunately, the Worcester area was often rainy, so it was better to walk in the rain. Our team also spent more time with each other in Worcester than we had in PE. As a result, even among the team members, we became annoyed with each other due to trivial things and talked with each other less.

When outreach was in progress, my diary said: 'Outreach is a mirror that reflects my heart. My heart was upset. It responds inadequately to leaders and team members. It is the mirror which reflects the anger, rebellion against authority, criticism and pride in me. Thank God and praise to the Lord for showing me these things.' Even though I wrote this, but my heart was upset and it was difficult to control. But now that several years have passed, when I think about it, I am very ashamed of my immature self. He was a leader who faithfully did his best in the region for many years even in the midst of hardship, but I didn't know him. And I was really narrow-minded about my teammates. I regret that I hadn't applied what I heard in the lecture while controlling my emotions at that time. As Ashley advised during the 8th week of lectures, when I dealt with other cultures, it would have been better if I had gone beyond my own culture and treated my team members with common sense and consideration... But my mind was narrow and my thoughts were short.

Anyway, meanwhile my bronchial symptoms, which

were stimulated by the air pollution in PE, became worse and worse. My cough worsened, too, and I couldn't sleep all night. I took all the medicine that I had prepared in South Korea, so I didn't have any more. Finally, I had to go to the hospital where the staff introduced Dr. Luke. His wife is Esther who gave a lecture for our 6th week lectures. The waiting room was full of patients, and the tall doctor was busy there. It was my turn. His office was neat and bright. Because I couldn't use my voice, my husband explained the symptoms. Dr. Luke looked down my throat, listened to my breathing using a stethoscope, and this and that. He looked at me for a while, and suddenly he smiled. Then he said, "When God has you lay down your work and then has you do it again, you will be stronger than before." And he told both of us to have hobbies. I thought 'Hmm? What is he talking about?' But I was sick and miserable, so I took the medicine, returned to the base, and forgot what he said. Thankfully, the symptoms slowly subsided after taking the medicine, and I could rejoin the ministry. Two months passed in the meantime, and outreach was over.

All the DTS students came back from outreach and got back together. However, Mozambique and Europe teams also did not have a good atmosphere. The air was quiet enough to feel heavy. The debriefing instructor, Andrew, carefully examined everyone's moods and proceeded with the class.

The outreach period was the time to practice what you had learned. And it seemed like it was time to realize how weak and fragile I was. By the grace of the Lord, if we prayed for the sick, they were healed. Many people felt

God's grace when we shared our life stories. It was full of rewarding and meaningful things. But on the other hand, it was also time to see how we would become upset because of our different cultures and our fragile characters that were still under construction. My feelings were easily shaken by nothing!! It wasn't easy to see how shallow my personality was. Oh! No!! The first day of debriefing, it was written in my lecture notes. *God! What should I do when I am disappointed with someone with whom I have high expectations and when I am disappointed with myself?* It seemed like the other teams weren't having an easy time either. Victor said with sadness in class. "Now this DTS is over, we may never see each other again." But we were still too weak like children to listen to Victor and cover up each other's faults, and we needed more time to broaden our minds.

During the debriefing period, students were relieving accumulated stress in their own way. Boys who liked soccer played soccer. When they were kicking the ball, the passion was hotter than the World Cup! Joshua and I met up with friends. Among them, Tom and Jacqueline came from Brazil, a great couple. Tom was an expert in technology and able to fix computers. My husband and Tom both loved ginger cookies. When they met each other, they talked about the ginger cookies they had found in South Africa and fixing computers. Computer and Ginger Cookies! These two topics made them friends. We invited this couple to our room. The menu was chosen as a pizza. My husband and I went to the mall and bought frozen pizza and fruits. It was a small meal with friends whom we invited to our room, but it was a good time.

Fortunately, by the end of the week, I was relieved of the emotions that had accumulated inside me, and I lifted my eyes that were focused on myself and looked up to the Lord. Thanksgiving to the Lord flowed out of my heart again. How the Lord comforted our South African team during the outreach period! Most of the team members did not have enough outreach expenses, so they ministered with anxiety. From the GAP church in Port Elizabeth to the farms in the Worcester area, our team was fed with various delicious foods including beef and chicken braai (South African barbecue) at many places we visited. I sincerely thank Instructor Andrew for giving us thoughtful and good lectures during the debriefing so that we could deal with each other's accumulated feelings and our disappointment and look at the Lord again. And how much the staff must have interceded for us! I'm really grateful.

Under the guidance and influence of Victor, our Awakening DTS students had awakened in the Lord while reflecting on our pasts. But Victor said that the person who needed the most faith was himself. In fact, as DTS leader, it was a worrying situation because less than half of the people had the admission fees and residence fees. He said that accepting these applicants in itself was a test of faith in the Lord who will supply all our needs. Surprisingly, all but one out of a total of 22 students graduated and completed the DTS. One student, who was an exception, left even though he was urged to stay. Faithful Lord!! Victor testified this during the debriefing time. And thank you to Victor and all the staff members who worked so hard!

On the day the debriefing was over, we went out after a long time to celebrate the last day. We went to the supermarket in the village near the base! It was a beautiful day with a blue and sunny sky. There was a vivid rainbow in the sky at the entrance of the market. And it was a double rainbow. Rainbows are common in Worcester. However, it was not a rainy day, and the perfect arch-shaped double rainbow was not common. A local resident nearby also mentioned that rainbows like this were rare. It was a rainbow bonus that the Lord especially showed us that we had done a great job!! We each bought ice cream and enjoyed it.

Now that I thought I'll be leaving this place in a few days, I wanted to store the familiar landscape in my memory. On the way back to the base, the village road, the winding hill road, the beautiful base scenery where the sky looks cool was engraved in my minds eye. Oh! There are animals that I want to remember. They are birds that lived in a big tree on the base grass field. They were similar to small ostriches, with dark earthy brown and thick feathers. These birds were large and were hairless, clear sky blue skin on their heads and long necks. I don't know what they are called. They looked unique, but what's more interesting was that they flew vertically up to the nest at the top of a big tree. If they flap their wings, they go straight up. *There's this kind of bird in the world!* The world, the animals and plants that the Lord has created seem to be beyond our imagination!

CHAPTER 18

Graduation & a New Start

November 21, the day of graduation. Awakening DTS held a graduation ceremony in a special place. It was a large wooden house with a wide garden. Inside the house, beautiful and pretty utensils were neatly placed on the long white table, and there was a nice chandelier upon the ceiling. Under the clear blue sky, graduates dressed up in formal clothes, and the ADTS staff all gathered to have a graduation dinner. Awakening DTS aims to awaken people to their identity in the Father and then guide them into their callings. True to that goal, ADTS had a profound impact on me who did this for the first time and my husband who did it again-My husband did the DTS with me again for his wife who did not do DTS. It was a time to congratulate and be joyful for each other for finishing ADTS well. We all enjoyed the atmosphere of the celebration and had a nice, delicious meal. Victor gave a toast, and we all cheered. Then we took a graduation photo together in the beautiful green garden. That's how the Worcester Base's first Awakening DTS officially ended.

One by one, the students returned to their hometowns and their respective places of life. The base became quiet like a school on vacation. Joshua and I stayed at the base for five more days before leaving. Anna and Linda also hadn't started leaving yet either. Besides cleaning the bathroom at the dorm, there was no work duty, and we had a few days to relax! We decided to make seafood pasta as a special meal. We went to the mall and bought imported frozen seafood. Squid and mussels - It's been a while since I've seen you!! My husband showed his cooking skills and made seafood spaghetti. It was delicious~

We packed a separate bowl of spaghetti and went to Anna and Linda's room. Fortunately, they were in the room. But both of them seemed to be out of energy. It could be because they said good-bye with their friends, or because the real world would be difficult to face again in the future. We handed them seafood spaghetti. The delicious scent stimulated their noses, and the mood seemed to get better. Linda was the chosen child of her tribe. In other words, she was raised to be the shaman of her tribe's religion. There were foods that were forbidden for the chosen child, and seafood was one of those prohibited foods. On this day, Linda broke a lifelong taboo, and she ate seafood - mussels - for the first time in her life, proclaiming the name of Jesus before us and Anna. It was the moment when freedom was declared in the Lord, and Satan's lies were broken. We all celebrated Linda's courage and rejoiced.

In the meantime, we had prayed for what to do next. From the time we were preparing for DTS in Korea, my husband and I had been thinking about a long-term mission for 4-5 years. So we got a South Africa visa for three years. However, we received a response from the Lord to move from South Africa to somewhere else. We wanted to stay for a long time because we came to like the Worcester Base, and there were many good programs... 'Lord! Where should we go?' The Lord gave us a heart to go north, and Sweden was among them through dreams, words, and the circumstantial environment from the past few weeks.

'Sweden? There were four bases in Sweden. Which of these should we go to?' My husband was searching about the bases on the internet.

"Look at this for a second," my husband said in an excited voice. There was a wide snowy forest of fir trees on the laptop screen! It was very similar to the scenery I saw in my dreams in South Korea. It is the northernmost of the four bases - Vilhelmina Base. It was amazing! We sent an email to the base leader.

After a while, we were contacted that they would accept us as short-term applicants. Vilhelmina Base was a small place with only one director couple and one staff. The temperature dropped to below -30 to -40 degrees Celsius (-22 to -40 degrees Fahrenheit) in winter there. 30 degrees below zero! I couldn't imagine the temperature 30 degrees below zero. *And it must be expensive because it's Europe...It's burdensome. What is God's will to lead us to a place with only 3 staff in the middle of winter?* I wondered, but when Joshua searched on the internet and found out that it was a mission center 150 years ago, hearing that, I began to look forward to it despite the pressure.

QT 3 days before leaving South Africa. Luke 5: 2-10. Peter ended up washing the net on the ground after overnight fishing. When Peter thinks it's not time to catch fish, Jesus tells him to go back to the deep water. But when he was obedient to Jesus, he caught so much fish that two boats would almost sink. Going to Sweden in the middle of winter seemed too burdensome... However, when meditating on the Word, my expectations for the Lord leading there grew.

In preparation for a new start, Joshua and I were busy. We had a lot of work to do: organizing our luggage, submitting our documents, and so on. The base staff decided to drive us to the airport. Anna and Linda saw us off as we left the base. I can still remember the scene of their last appearance through the car window. Goodbye, Linda! Goodbye, Anna! May the Lord's grace be with you and see you again. Until then, stay healthy…We said goodbye to our dear friends and Worcester Base.

◆ **Letter to Dream team and Friends - November 24, 2013**

Hello~ We graduated on the November 21 after completing all five months of the Awakening DTS course. From the day after graduation, our friends who we trained with together started going home. I'm excited about the new beginning, and I'm sorry to say goodbye to my friends and friendly base.

Yesterday, we took our French friend Miriam to the airport, and something interesting happened on the way there. Miriam is from Madagascar and studied in France 30 years ago and became a school teacher there. Now she had a vision of Christian counseling in her home country of Madagascar, and she quit school and came to DTS training.

To get to the airport from Worcester, we have to go through big mountain and long tunnels, where wild baboons live. Baboons are bigger than monkeys and smaller than orangutans. When we passed here, Joshua saw a baboon twice, and each time I was looking for them, "Where? Where?", but I missed the opportunity and couldn't see them. Now I am leaving South Africa in two days, and I prayed to God because I desperately wanted to see a baboon today. *"Lord! I've been upset because I missed the chance to see a baboon many times. I really hope to see it today. But my eyes are bad, so I can't see a baboon even when it is on the side of the road. So I hope the baboon can be in a place where I can see it for sure."* And if the Lord answered my prayers, I am not going to miss it this time, and I was looking out the window and talking to Miriam in the back seat.

Suddenly, Joshua stepped on the brakes and shouted, "Baboon!" And in front of the car we were in, not one baboon but a baboon family of seven or nine was crossing the road!! Dad, mom, baby, brother, and sister baboon~ The baboon family of all sizes were slowly walking across the road in a line, just in front of the car. They came to a fence across from the road and sat in a row. "Wow~!!" Laughter and exclamations exploded from everyone. Miriam, who was in the back seat, was happy, saying, "I think God is winking now." God responded immediately to my little prayer that I wanted to see a baboon. He called the baboon family and made them cross the road at the right time. My faith grew rapidly, thanks to God who took care of us like this. Even now, when I think about the scene, it makes me smile. I think it was also a great encouragement to Miriam, who was preparing for the next step of counseling school in Oregon, USA.

Looking back on all our journeys, ADTS and life in South Africa, I think everything is God's grace.

During 40 days of special early morning prayer, my heart heated up through *Pilgrim's Progress*. Then God gave me the desire to do DTS on the 35th day. With the help of God

...Our house was sold in 3 days. I was able to resign from my job. I could tell my younger brother and my parents about going to South Africa. We received prayers and farewell from our beloved Dream Team. We had a good relationship with the missionaries in Cambodia. The Lord guided us to depart a week ahead of schedule, to protect us from the worst wildfire in Indonesia. God holds our body and mind so that we could adapt well in South Africa, and train our soul to become stronger through ADTS. God blessed us so that we could meet faithful Korean missionaries, YWAM staff, and DTS friends here.

Above all, I can feel the love of God in my heart...

There are so many times of appreciation that the cultural shock and environmental difficulties that I initially felt here no longer were difficulties. I am still tired from my busy schedule, but I feel good and happy when I summed up the past six months. Thank you very much, Lord.

Yesterday, we had meals and fellowship at the house of missionary Kim, who works hard in the educational field. His wife made us Tteokbokki for lunch. It had been 6 months since I ate Tteokbokki! The taste was great! I ate two bowls~ In addition, the missionary gave us a down parka that comes down to my knees and two underclothes. I was grateful to see that the unexpected needs were met, and I remembered the small cloud the Lord showed Elijah. And we have a little faith in God, who will warm us up and protect us even in Sweden's strong cold. So I try to focus more on God's heart that leads me there than worrying about what to wear or what to eat.

After 24 hours, we leave South Africa and head north.

Please intercede for us to get healthier, have a good relationship with people we meet in Sweden, and to serve Europe as a channel of blessing to share God's love and grace. Thank you for supporting us with intercession, warm encouragement, and love. We pray that God's peace and grace will always be with you. With our last greetings from South Africa...

Joshua and Heejin ~~

Pastor Tata James was called by God a year and a half after his DTS, and Missionary Kim passed away after devoting himself to education ministry in South Africa. I remember them with special respect.

Figure 6. Hello ~ Miriam, Heejin, and Joshua

PART IV. SECOND STEP

From Worcester, South Africa
to Seamill Base, Glasgow, UK

CHAPTER 19

British Seamill Base

From the southern tip of sunny South Africa, to Northern Europe close to Greenland! To go to Sweden in the middle of winter, it was necessary to adapt to the weather. So we decided to stay in Scotland's Seamill base for about 10 days. We went from Glasgow to a small seaside town with a base. It rained lightly. While wandering on the road for a while, the sun set and became dark. In an unfamiliar place, I was scared. At that time, there was the sound of a person behind us. Who was it? Thankfully, it was a woman who was on her way to the base. She introduced herself as Intercession Team member Sarah. As we followed her, the base was immediately visible after a while. The Seamill Base was a small stone castle.

I experienced the British weather that I only heard in words. It rained several times a day, and the sky was cloudy with the chilly temperature, and the sun set at about 4 o'clock. I didn't think much of rooibos tea, which was so delicious in the hot South African sunlight. Instead, the black tea was really delicious. In Korea, I drink it once in a while, but the change in my taste for tea over a few days seems to be due to the weather. I understand why the British love to drink black tea.

A few days later, Joshua and I went to the post office in a nearby village when it wasn't raining. I wanted to send postcards and cards because it was Christmas soon. We stopped by the post office and started doing my favorite thing when going to a new place: exploring the neighborhood! We went around the village along the main road. It was a quiet, small, and cozy place. The villagers were friendly even when they saw unfamiliar Asians. Maybe it's because the base had many visitors. I seemed to know why my husband recommended the Seamill Base.

When we were there, the base was quiet because it was the vacation period after a school had finished. Still, we could meet many people on the base during mealtime. They said that soon there will be a Christmas party at the base. We perked up. Oh ~ a party?! My husband asked if there was 'Eggnog' at the party. The answer was yes. My husband was very happy. It was the first time I've ever heard of it. What is eggnog? My husband excitedly said that it was a Christmas drink made by mixing eggs and something. For reference, my husband enjoys food as much as I do. They also said they would decorate the Christmas tree the evening before the party. We also wanted to help with something, so we went to decorate it for Christmas. When we went, people were gathering here and there to make tree decorations. We cut paper together, decorated a tree with a long paper chain, and took a picture in front of it! We had a small but pleasant Christmas dinner party with the rest of the base family. My husband and I had a good time, too.

And we heard more good news. A few days later, there would be a Christmas festival in town! Yeah! All small town shops were open, and prepared snacks were given to customers who visited the shop. And of course, it was free!!!! We went to a festival with Sarah, who had helped us when we were lost. We went around the village together, saw a beautifully decorated Christmas tree, ate delicious snacks, and most of all, drank a traditional

Christmas drink made with hot wine. It was the first traditional Scottish Christmas drink I tasted, and the wine drink from which the alcohol was steamed off, was perfect for soothing my body in a chilly winter filled with moisture. Christmas at the Seamill Base was full of fun! Thank you, Sarah, for taking care of us~

As we were dining with the base staff, they found out that we were going to the Vilhelmina Base in Sweden. When they heard us mention the Vilhelmina base, they were very happy. They were all friends of Vilhelmina Base's staff member, John, because he had previously been at the Seamill Base. In this case, the world is very small. Everyone, including Sarah, missed John and asked us to say hello to him. As the LORD confirmed through the Seamill Base people that this journey was in the right direction, much of my anxiety disappeared.

CHAPTER 20

Vilhelmina, Sweden

December 9. We departed from England and arrived in Copenhagen, Denmark. We waited five hours to change planes and arrived in Stockholm, Sweden. The next day, we took a small propeller plane to the northern city of Vilhelmina. The base director Paul was there to meet us. Paul drove skillfully on a snow-covered road. Arriving at the base, we had tea with the directors Paul and Emily and staff member John. John guided us to the accommodation. It was a small red two-story house made of wood. John gave way for us and moved so that we can stayed on the first floor. Sweden's Vilhelmina was a place with an average temperature of -30 degrees Celsius (-22°F) in winter. My husband had no clothes to withstand this cold. When we decided to go to Sweden in South Africa, I sent an urgent email to Casablanca in South Korea. She sent me a thick coat that Joshua could wear in Antarctica. When I came to the base, the coat arrived two days earlier than we did. But strangely, the temperature outside was tolerable. Paul said that temperatures had risen to minus 5 degrees Celsius (23°F) from 2-3 days before we arrived.

The day after we arrived, Joshua and I decided to go to the village with John. John said he would buy the pieces of heating wood for the base. *What kind of wood for heating?* I got curious about what kind of place was selling it. And we needed to go to the Salvation Army to buy winter supplies, such as gloves and hats, which we couldn't find at the base boutique in the morning (many YWAM bases have a place called the 'boutique'. There are items donated by students and staff when they leave the base, and those who need them can take them for free. So this is one of the popular places among YWAMers). And we decided to meet the church member who had a dinner appointment with John, eat together, and watch a movie at the town hall. In the frozen kingdom, we must be prepared to go out.

We shared with John, Seamill Base's greetings. John was happy. How did American John come to northern Sweden? The clue was in his last name. John had an unusual surname as an American, but in fact his ancestors were Swedish. Although he was born and raised in the United States, Swedish history was flowing in his blood. He felt the Lord's guidance to Sweden, and he felt comfortable in Sweden. Perhaps that's why John was an important leader among the local church youth, even though it was a short period of a year in Sweden. The young man who decided to eat dinner was also a man discipled by John in the church. Even when we went to the theater to see *The Hobbit*, we met and greeted the young church members who welcomed John. The next day Joshua went out to repair the broken windows with Paul. In the meantime, I organized our luggage. In the evening, there was a Bible study for young people. We also went to Mission Church, where the base served along with Paul and John.

Soon after, Casablanca informed me that the 40 days special early morning prayer would begin soon. The theme was Amazing Grace!! We needed the Lord's grace. The subject touched my heart. In anticipation of the wonderful grace of the Lord, we also decided to join it. Due to the time difference, we decided to give one hour of special prayer instead of the early morning worship service. And I chose the subject of prayer with the heart of expectation. We asked the Lord about our missionary journey. And we asked for guidance concerning how long we should be in Sweden and where we are going to next.

Next to the base was a small school building for Sami children, which had operated until the 1940s. The Sami are a minority ethnic group living in northern Scandinavia by raising reindeer. In the late 1800s, there was a Sami woman who asked the Swedish king to build a school for Sami children. The school was built by the king because the king was moved by the woman who went on a wooden ski for 1,000 kilometers (621 miles) from Northern Sweden to Stockholm. Many missionaries devoted themselves as teachers to provide education for the Sami children. However, after tuberculosis turned up in the 1940s, the school was moved to another place, the building was abandoned. This is the "Mission Center" we saw in South Africa.

I felt like we should go around this school building for a week like the Israelites had done around Jericho to pray. The next day, we went round this building like a Jericho castle. We did that every day for 6 days. And it was the last day. On that day, we decided to go around seven times, but when I looked outside, there was a snowstorm. We wore layers of clothing, knee-length woolen socks, boots we bought at a second-hand store, and finally a fur hat covering our ears. We were fully armed! Ready to go!! We began to go around the snowfields where snow were well above our knees. One, two,… and in the last seven laps, I prayed earnestly that God would give revival to the northern Scandinavians and the Sami. A few days later, when I read the Bible, I was comforted by Zechariah 6:8 "Then he called to me, "Look, those going toward the north country have given my Spirit rest in the land of the north." I still didn't know why we had to come here, but these words gave me comfort and made me think, "It wasn't in vain that we came here."

There was something I liked in northern Sweden. Making a fire in the fireplace! How fun this was!! Split firewood that was piled up outside would be piled up on the front porch of the house in advance when the weather was good. The door to the house was double doored to prevent cold air. And the firewood stacked on the porch would be placed in a firewood box next to the inner door and dried for 2-3 days. If the firewood dries well enough to prevent smoke from burning, it's ready. First, pile the firewood in the fireplace so that it can air well, then put a starter underneath that looks like a small sawdust, finally light the paper to light the starter. How fun it is to light firewood! When I was young, I liked playing with fire. I used to like playing with matches secretly so that my mom didn't know~

One night there was a big winter storm in northern Sweden. The wind caused great damage to the full-grown trees that were about to be cut down and sold. Fortunately, there was not much storm damage near the YWAM base, but there were still a few fallen trees as I walked along the road. But something strange caught my eye. They were large trees that grew up toward the sky but they had few roots. There were roots, but they grew sideways, not downward. It was different from the trees I had seen so far. The tree grows for many decades and stretches upward, but the roots were very shallow. This area is wet and snowy. Since the area is always rich in water, the tree didn't have to take deep roots. So when the wind blows, the trees easily fall.

As I thought of the trees, I suddenly thought of a Korean poem. 'The deep-rooted tree will not be shaken by the wind…' In life, there are times when we get thirsty due to lack of water. I hope the Lord will shower down quickly, but there is no news about rain even if I pray earnestly. I felt disappointment and sometimes blamed Him. Still, looking back at the past, I think that's when I took root in faith and found groundwater the Lord gave me. Seeing the fallen firs that day, I learned the benefits of patiently putting down roots in the Lord in the midst of hope even when the drought came. Deep-rooted trees can stand even if there are wind storms.

◆ **Letter to Dream team and Friends - December 29, 2013**

Happy New Year 2013~We have 53 hours and 15 minutes left in 2013! I think it's time to say, "Adieu" (goodbye forever) to 2013, looking back on this year. When I was in my early 30s, I didn't know God well and hadn't yet met my beloved church friends and missionaries, and I was filled with loneliness. I was more lonely during the Christmas holidays. Now that there are many friends in faith, the holidays are no longer cold and lonely. Thank you, God

In northern Sweden, there have been several revivals since

the late 12th century, so Christian culture is deeply embedded in everyday life. Before and after Christmas, seven candles (or candle-shaped bulbs) symbolizing seven churches, as well as the Christmas tree, are decorated on the windows of every house. Then the candles beautifully light up the darkness of winter, which has gone dark within five hours after sunrise. There's a drink that seems to be mixed with cinnamon in a coke that only comes out on Christmas, and there is a traditional Christmas bread, sweets and pies. So you can see from traditional food that Christmas is really a special day.

We were invited to a Swedish family's home to eat together this holiday season. This family are grateful sisters who have helped in many ways since the base directors Paul and Emily came here ten years ago. The older sister's family, the younger sister's family, and about 20 friends from the village were together. It was a small party where we made 2-3 dishes at home and brought them, ate together, and shared gifts worth about 10 dollars.

Emily made three dessert pies, one of which I made with Emily (as an assistant) a traditional Swedish nut pie. First, we gathered together at the older sister's house and had a nice meal, and we moved to the younger sister's house and had Christmas drinks, coffee, and pies made by Emily, talked about this and that, and shared gifts that were the highlight. They invited unbelieving village friends to spend a happy time together and wisely delivered Luke 2:14 "Glory to God in the highest heaven, and on earth peace to those on whom his favor rests." I was very grateful that Joshua and I could have a warm Christmas party with a Swedish Christian family.

The next day, on December 25, we had an English-style

Christmas dinner at the invitation of Englishman Paul and the Dutch Emily. Just like the cultures of Korea, Japan, and China, are different in the same northeast Asia, I realized the culture of each country in Europe is different from each other even just in their food. John also had a great time together with us. Although there were various cultures, it was very nice to see all of them sharing Jesus' birth with rich and special food.

Just before the start of the Christmas holiday, there was something hopeful about the fellowship and unity between the Christian youth here. The Vilhelmina base staff have been praying for the young people for the past year, opening café on Friday and Saturday evenings on the first floor of Mission Church. Just before this Christmas, young people from the largest church in the area filled the café and had a great time. It was all God's grace.

There aren't many people I've met in this sparsely populated area, but there are some really impressive significant ones. One of them is a small elderly woman who came to visit us when the weekend café was open. She is a member of the church next door, and she said she wanted to see us. She told us about a vision she had seen before. It was amazing to hear that the Lord's finger came down from heaven and touched the earth. I could see that she had a passion for the Lord and a strong desire for revival.

And now, as I'm writing this letter, a Church Association Youth Retreat in Northern Scandinavia is being held for four nights and five days. Unfortunately, we don't know Swedish so we couldn't go with the staff. Instead, we are doing a very important ministry protecting the base of

Vilhelmina - intercession and heating. In Sweden, in the middle of winter, water pipes burst easily in the cold even when the heating system is on. So we held down the fort so that the base staff could concentrate on the ministry in peace.

It will be 2014 soon. I think many of you will have a passionate year-end with 40-day special early morning prayer and year-end worship. I hope you will enjoy the rest of your time in grace. I pray that the New Year will be double the grace and peace of the Lord.

From Joshua and Heejin at Vilhelmina, Sweden~

Shortly after we started praying about what we should do in the future, Revelation 11:1 appeared during QT. "Go and measure the temple of God and the altar, with its worshipers." More prayer was needed for discernment. When 2013 was less than a few days left, and the last day we went to the Sami school, John 14:31 "Come now; let us leave." touched our hearts. Originally, our plan was to stay here for at least a year. But our hearts and the words we were given were different. The cloud arose faster than we had thought, so we had to pack up again. Now our prayer topic became, "Then where do we go?"

During the Northern Scandinavian Church Union Youth Retreat, the few days Joshua and I kept the base, the two of us celebrated the New Year. I was at the large dining table in the kitchen and read the Word. And I saw the saying, "to celebrate the Festival of Tabernacles." We prayed together about what to do. Our hearts came together that Israel was the next destination. And the purpose of going is to pray. But I got caught up in the phrase "the Festival of Tabernacles." Is this the festival of building and living in booths made with tree branches for a week?! I assumed, *It's probably difficult to stay in Israel during this time...*

The leader couple and John returned. From the bright and lively appearance of Emily, I felt that there was grace at the retreat. In the meeting together, we also talked about what had happened in the meantime. We said goodbye to the friendly Swedish Mission Church. Paul and Emily told us to come next time when the weather was nice in July and August and not in the middle of winter. In the summer, people sleep in the cabin watching the stars, and during the day they fish in the lake and fry the fish in butter. Wow!! My husband and I were sent off by Paul and set out for Israel.

About a week later, an email came from Paul. After we left, the temperature again dropped to -30 degrees Celsius (-22°F). The temperature, which rose 2-3 days before we arrived, ranged from minus 5-14 degrees Celsius (23~6.8°F) while we were there. It was really fortunate that the temperature rose for Joshua and me, who were vulnerable to the cold, but the farms that raised reindeer in northern Sweden were worried. When the temperature again dropped to -30 degrees Celsius, their concerns also "dropped." The temperature was abnormal for a while during the month we were there. It was a wonderful timing from the Lord. A coat from Casablanca that my husband could use in Antarctica was left at the base boutique for someone who will come there next.

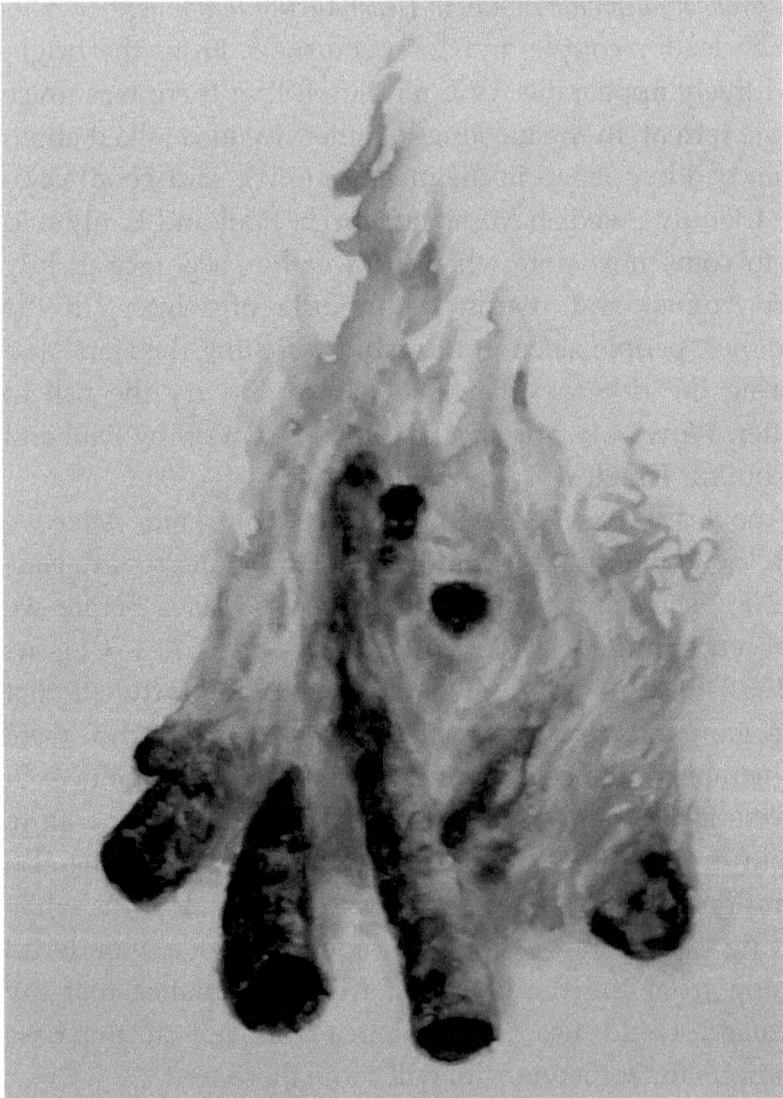

Figure 7. Campfire in Vilhelmina, Sweden

CHAPTER 21

Continental Europe

The way we went to Israel was not through a direct route. The next destination was Israel, but we didn't go directly and instead went through Europe. We put our heads together to discuss it. And decided on the following principles. 1. According to Genesis 13:17 'Go, walk through the length and breadth of the land', we decided to go stop by as many countries as we could. 2. Use low cost airlines and public transportation to save money. 3. Stay at the YWAM bases where we are in contact with the hospitality staff. 4. And we decided to go to the Eastern European YWAM base near the route.

My husband found a good and affordable airline. And he contacted the bases. We were able to get connected to Amsterdam (in the Netherlands), Milan (in Italy) and Czech staff. So, according to the airline's event special route, Amsterdam, Milan, trains to Switzerland/France, Israel, Germany, Czech Republic by bus, Amsterdam by airline. This is how our travel plan was formed. From South Africa to Scotland then to Sweden, so far, the food is rich and the people are generous. From now on, a higher level of minimal life training is expected. Our penny-pinching journey was beginning!!

We arrived in Amsterdam on January 7, 2014. We took a long train ride from the airport to the center of the city and arrived at the destination. We followed the map on Google and found the YWAM Amsterdam base. It was a large building in the middle of the city. We knocked on a large brown door made of thick wood. Two young men opened the door inside. The room we stayed in had a good view of the outside. Across the street there was a place like a museum. In front of our room there were three or four white, pretty swans in the small waterway. The joy of seeing wonderful and beautiful white swans. 'Ah~~Pretty'.

The next morning, we walked around the neighborhood near the base. We had a good time looking around the base and seeing a shop that sells round cheese the size of a millstone. Afterwards we had to go back to the airport because our luggage arrived a day late. Fortunately, we found our luggage, and it was safe. We had to go to Milan the next morning, so we got accommodation near the airport. The 2 days and 1 night stay was short, but Amsterdam Base was a lively place. I want to go there again if I have a chance. Each of us had a large suitcase and a backpack. The suitcases were burdensome because we had to move to many countries in a short time. When I asked the manager of the Ibis hotel, he said he could keep our luggage for a month. I was relieved to see that there was a separate room for them, and many others had left behind their luggage too. I was very grateful to be able to leave the heavy loads.

On January 10, we left the hotel with a backpack on, and departed for Milan by plane at 9:25 a.m. The base area was like a new town with lots of apartment complexes. Not long after it was started, the Milan Base was growing with the help of two bases near its area. The base was made of two floors that connected the upper and lower floors of an apartment with narrow spiral stairs. Downstairs there was a kitchen, a living room, a conference room, and a lodging house with bunk beds. There was a guest room and other accommodation upstairs. As we arrived, Susan, who was in charge of hospitality, welcomed us. Susan made her very-own tomato spaghetti and served us dinner. Two or three staff members at the dorm also came and said hello, and we had a good time together. They gave us a room for the school instructors, and we were so thankful. When I entered the room, I found a sincere welcome box with snacks and candy. Even though it may have been difficult because it is a small base, I was impressed by the way they welcomed us with all their sincerity according to YWAM's principle of 'Hospitality'.

At mealtime the next day, there was announced a "Milan Region Church Unity Special Prayer Meeting" at the square in front of the Duomo Cathedral on Sunday. My husband and I also decided to attend the prayer meeting. We went before the appointed time and looked around the Duomo Cathedral. It was a magnificent and beautiful cathedral with elaborate sculptures on the walls. In time, people began to gather in front of the cathedral. There were about 100-150 people.

I said to Joshua, "We're just visitors, so let's just pray quietly in the back row." My husband nodded. But...the leader who was leading in front suddenly said, "Everyone turn around!!... Let's kneel on the floor and pray together in prayer loudly!" 'Huh? This is not what I wanted...' My husband and I unexpectedly came to pray in the front row. We were sitting awkwardly, and thinking, *How did it become like this? Anyway...Let's pray hard.* We kneeled on the floor. I closed my eyes and prayed aloud in tongues, and my heart grew hot. After the prayers, we were feeling well like people who had done something meaningful. And we got on the tram that I had only seen in the movies, looked around the city, even the alleys, and returned to base. Monday, the next day was a regular meeting day for the Milan base. Joshua and I also participated. The leader was smiling at us. 'Um~~why??' After a while, he showed a video from the prayer meeting the day before. 'Oh! Those two guys are very familiar!!' In Milan, the city of fashion, we wore navy and red parkas worn with baggy pants- far from the fashion found in the city. We found them in the Swedish YWAM boutique. 'Right in the front row... It's really so noticeable...'

Talking about fashion, how strange we must have looked at the time... an embarrassing fashion sense. Fake EasyJet coat named by My husband. He was searching for a low-cost airline and found EasyJet. It showed something interesting, an EasyJet Coat. It was a well-made trench coat. What's unusual was the hidden pockets that can hold 24 items. If the weight and size of the bag exceed the regulations, there is an extra charge, so this ingenious coat came out. We benchmark this pretty functional coat!! Fleece, padded vest, and down parka in three layers. (1 inside pocket + 2 outside pockets) x 3 layers= 9 pockets in total. I put as much stuff as I could fit in a total of nine pockets. To describe the shape as cutely as possible, a squirrel holds a full acorn on both cheeks. I was a little worried about taking off my clothes while checking at the airport. Whether it was the generosity of the people, they didn't know the size of Asians, or they overlooked us, they passed us through. Together, we earned at least 5 kgs (11 pounds)~

We spent three nights and four days in Milan. To catch the EasyJet to Israel, we took the 11 am train from Milan to

Switzerland. Across the border, soldiers with guns on the train asked me to show them my passport. I showed my passport reflexively in surprise and put it in my bag, which made me feel strange. South Korea is like an island where the three sides of the east, west, and south have huge oceans, and North Korea is in the North. If I want to go to China, I have to fly in and out of the airport. In Europe, I do it on a train. If Korea is unified by the grace of the Lord someday, it will be the day when we can go to China on a train too.

We arrived in Switzerland on the afternoon of January 13. As I had walked around for half a day, I was thirsty. 'Where can I buy water?' Thankfully, there was a convenience store. In our tight budget, water was also expensive, so it was even difficult to get thirsty often in Europe. But did I see the price properly? In Korea, Evian is very expensive, but 1 liter is only 1 dollar! After our DTS, it had been a long time since my husband had generously bought something for me. I grabbed two liters of Evian in my arms and walked happily without even knowing it was heavy.

The flight to Israel was early in the morning, and we had to go to the airport at dawn. So my husband booked our accommodation 10 minutes away from the airport. It was an less expensive guesthouse in France right next to the Swiss border. I was a little worried because it was my first time in a guest house, but the exterior was neat, there were at least 20 rooms on one floor, and the size looked good. We opened the door to our room. It was a cool wallpaper with blue stripes, a bunk bed, but it looked neat. 'Hmm~I think I like it. So far ok! I felt a little reassured. Next was the important toilet check! But...'Where's the restroom?'

The two of us searched for a long time and finally found it! A unisex restroom in front of the central stairs and one shower room next to it! That was all for one floor!! Besides, I had to put in a coin in every time I used the toilet...Oh... my husband... saves too much!!... Enjoying the Evian was so short-lived.

Fortunately, that night passed safely...January 15 at 7:20 a.m. We boarded the EasyJet which we bought on a special sale and left for Israel!!

CHAPTER 22

Israel, Jerusalem

We arrived at the Tel Aviv Airport on January 15. We left the airport after completing the immigration process and asked where we could take the bus to Jerusalem. There seemed to be no bus stop, but there were a few people standing by the side of the road. The people we met on the street kindly informed us. Then a bus was coming from far away. The two of us just ran, fortunately, we got on the bus just in time. We rode the bus for about an hour. The bus went up the yellow dirt road, and we stopped at a building parking lot. I thought it was a rest stop, but we had already arrived. We were in Jerusalem!!!

My husband searched on the Internet to find out where to pray according to the "message" to celebrate the Festival of Tabernacles and to pray in Jerusalem. Then, he found two houses of prayer that faithfully interceded for Israel. We decided to pray for two weeks with the heart of someone lighting one light a day in the seven cups of the lampstand in the temple. One of the houses of prayer was in a tall building in the old city of Jerusalem. It was said that this prayer room was built on the top of the building so that people could pray while looking at Jerusalem. The other prayer room was on the other side of the City of David so that people could pray while looking at the old city where the temple was located. To get there, we had to go downhill and then up to the village on the hill across from the city of David. We prayed, changing prayer houses one day at a time. When we went to the prayer room, people from all over the world were praying.

The part of the path we walked was down the walls of Jerusalem. As I passed by, I thought of visiting the place for a while, but I remembered my friend who had been on a pilgrimage to the Holy Land a few years ago. She was excited about the Via Dolorosa, but she was disappointed because it was a crowded and noisy market. But in fact, she received an answer to her prayers for a spouse, an important decision in her life on that trip. After listening to this friend's advice, my husband and I decided to go to Via Dolorosa after a lot of prayer. To prepare my heart, I read the Gospel of Mark with my husband, which explains in detail the suffering of Jesus on the cross.

The joy of arriving in Jerusalem lasted for only a little while. The expensive prices in Jerusalem surprised us! It is a holy land for Jews, Muslims and Christians around the world, including Catholics, Greek Orthodox, and Protestants, so the small city was full of people. It was fortunate that it was not the peak season. Eventually, for accommodation, my husband searched the Internet every day and moved to the cheapest place on that day. I understood why HE told us to celebrate the Festival of Tabernacles when HE told us about Israel as the next destination in Sweden. If it weren't for His word, I would have nagged my husband who booked the accommodation every morning.

Jerusalem was a mixture of Jews who had returned from many countries. The kinds of things in the market differed depending on where the people in the neighborhood lived and migrated from the world. In the Old City center where we stayed, there was a mart run by Russian immigrants. It was fun to see Russian food while buying water to drink there. We bought bread and fruits at the traditional market in Jerusalem. We bought seasonal fruits, which were available in plenty in January, and bread that looked like baked Hotteok (a Korean snack of flattened bread that was filled with a mix of sweet sugar and nuts and baked in oil). It was delicious when I dipped the flatbread into yogurt! While passing the market, we saw some dried peppers. I had needed red pepper powder, so it was good that the market had some. So we bought 500 grams of ground red pepper powder. We wanted to buy more, but we couldn't increase the weight of our luggage. But what we learned after we left Israel is that all agricultural products are organic. If we had known that, we would have bought three times more. In the Old City center where we stayed, there was a take-out restaurant similar to Subway. When we chose all kinds of stir-fried vegetables, the worker rolled them into a thin baked flour bread similar to a tortilla. In front of the delicious food, my husband opened our wallet, hahaha! It was so delicious that I want to eat it even now.

In the meantime, the 40-day special early morning prayer was over, and the two weeks in Jerusalem were almost over. On January 25, it was the day to go to the House of Prayer overlooking the city of Jerusalem. We came up after praying and went to the inner city of Jerusalem. There were narrow alleys and houses made of bright sand-colored stones. My husband looked at Jerusalem and remembered Revelation 11:1-2. "Go and measure the temple of God and the altar, with its worshipers. But exclude the outer court; do not measure it, because it has been given to the Gentiles. They will trample on the holy city for 42 months." It's a very sad word, but this word given through an angel came true. Is it because my husband's eyes directly confirmed that the words of the Bible became even more real? My husband said that his faith suddenly rose. Words seemed to have come to my husband's mind anew. I believe that the Lord who fulfills the Word will also fulfill the words of New Jerusalem in the rest of the book of Revelation in His time.

Then we headed for the Via Dolorosa. Even though my friend had mentioned that I shouldn't expect much, I couldn't help being excited about going. Upon arrival, the Via Dolorosa was an ordinary road similar to the other roads in David's city. The only difference was that there were Roman numeral plaques from 1 to 14 on the road, and the events that had happened there were briefly written down. Where Jesus was judged. It is now the front yard of a building. The place where Jesus fell while walking with the cross. *How do they know this even until now? Did Jesus really fall down here?* I thought. However, on the one hand, many people must have verified it, but I thought that the fact that the places are marked in such detail is evidence that it is an undeniable historical fact.

As the numbers went up, the road got narrower. Later, it became a narrow market road where two people in the group could not walk side by side. It was a small alley where people lived. A narrow market street with shops on both sides. As we followed the numbers, we thought about the related history. As it was the Jewish Sabbath, there were fewer people than usual, but the road was still crowded. It was fortunate that due to what my friend told me, I had given up my expectation that this place would have a holy atmosphere. But at that time, this thought came from a corner of my mind. *People were busy with their own work, and they didn't care what Jesus was doing. But for them, and for us, Jesus passed this road with a heavy cross.* When this thought came to mind, the noisy path of the market that I had just passed turned into a path of love where the Lord's sincere devotion could be felt. My heart was so moved.

At the last 10-14 stops on the Via Dolorosa was the place where Jesus was crucified and where there was a tomb. There was a small chapel for prayer in a large church built there. As I sat down for a moment and prayed, I remembered the word John 19:30 "It is finished." And I realized why God had brought me to Israel. I have heard about Jesus and the cross from a young age, so I took for granted that Jesus died on the cross for our sins. But it didn't touch my heart deeply, because His death on the cross was a part of Christian culture that was like air to me. I was not impressed with the cross of Jesus, as if my heart was veiled. But after seeing the Via Dolorosa, I believed in my heart that the Lord took my sin and went down the road just for me. On that very day, the cross of Jesus reached my heart. Remembering the Via Dolorosa...

The Way

The narrow stone road
The hard road
My heavy sins crush his shoulders
He held to the end and climbed
The way

The bumpy road
The lonely road
Even if your eyes are covered by the blood
From the piercing crown of thorns
You kept going and saying
I love you I love you I love you
The way

◆ Letter to Dream team and Friends - January 21, 2014

How have you been? In the meantime, we went from northern Sweden to Israel. There's been a big change! Joshua and I also prayed for an hour every day with the heart of joining for the 40-day special early morning prayer and prayed that God would lead our journey. But one day during QT, the word that I had to go to Israel for at least two weeks came to my heart. Over the next few days we were told to go to Jerusalem and gather together to intercede for Israel. So we changed our schedule and prepared to go to Israel in a hurry, and by the grace of God, we arrived safely in Jerusalem.

From the day after we arrived, we found two places to gather together and pray according to the word given. We went around the outside of the old Jerusalem to find these places and lodgings, and there was a large Mormon University and a mosque built on the Mount of Olives where Jesus prayed. Around 3 p.m., two mosques on the Mount of Olives and a mosque in the old temple site across from it were broadcasting prayers at the same time, and the whole area rang loudly.

This past Friday and Saturday I experienced what the Jewish Sabbath was like. Almost all the trams and cars were cut off from 3pm on Friday, and no traffic lights were needed on the streets because there were so few cars. There were many stores that were either already closed or preparing to close in haste. A little later, people dressed in black and wearing big hats went around and blew small trumpets. At 4:15 p.m., a siren that sounded like a trumpet went off, and literally all stores except for McDonalds and restaurants owned by non-Jews were closed from sunset on Friday to sunset on Saturday. The usually noisy city became quiet. It was impressive to see the whole community working hard to keep the Sabbath. The Jews' had great zeal to keep the

Sabbath.

On Sunday, we went to worship at a Messianic Jewish church. It was not big, but it was full of people who praised and worshiped passionately. I was so touched to see them worship. It was great to see the worship of Jewish people who believed in Jesus. They were peaceful, bright, and lively. I hope that the love of God who sent Jesus will be delivered soon to the Jews who do not yet believe in Jesus.

Many prophets in the Bible talked about Jerusalem's restoration, but in fact, I felt like it was someone else's business while reading the Bible until I came to Jerusalem. Until now, I had not been interested in Israel. But when I came to Israel, I was very sad to know that there was a history of painful acts committed by Christians. After the fall of Jerusalem by Rome, for more than 2,000 years, the Jews who lost their country and wandered have had a painful history involving Christians during those years.

I've been here for a few days and realize that Israel and Jerusalem really need a lot of prayer. During today's intercession, I was heartbroken and tearful as I remembered the reality that their wounds due to the past had become a thick wall to welcome Jesus. I ask you to intercede so that the river of the Holy Spirit will flow into Israel and Israel will be restored quickly. Thank you.

Heejin and Joshua from Jerusalem

Figure 8. The Cross & I (an engraving on wood)

CHAPTER 23

Israel, Holy Land

In the meantime, two weeks passed in Jerusalem. On January 30, we rented a car and went up to Galilee. Holding in the tourist instinct and desire, which I had held in so far, I decided to visit many places in Galilee. Israel can be reached from top to bottom by car in about 3 hours. Yet the road was surprisingly colorful. Within that short distance, the wilderness of red soil turned into a fresh green grassland. Wow!! I was wondering what kind of place Galilee was like? Galilee captivated us from the entrance! From the beginning of our arrival at Galilee, we felt refreshed.

There were many black stones around the Lake of Galilee. Old houses were also built of these black stones. I thought that this area could be a topography that was created by a volcanic eruption like the Caldera Lake-volcanic crater lake. Well, that's enough geography~ Anyway, I was excited. As soon as we unpacked our luggage, the two of us went to the Galilee Traditional Market. It had a similar atmosphere to Korean traditional markets. We toured the market and I looked for my wallet to buy some fruit. "Huh?!! Where is IT?" The wallet that I put in the front pocket of the jacket had disappeared!! A pickpocket! At that moment, I was stunned.The store owner looked at us with pitiful eyes. Ah~~ in this place called Holy Land... It seems like people are the same everywhere. I felt bad about my lost wallet, and felt upset about being pickpocketed. We quit shopping and took the bus back to the hotel.

But my sadness was only for a moment. I was relieved by the sunset reflected on the Lake of Galilee. Our lodging was an small older hotel on the way down to the Sea of Galilee. It was a place used by Russian pilgrims. For breakfast, a diet tailored to the tastes of the Russians came out. It was delicious. It was an inexpensive and practical accommodation where you could cook in your room. The owner was a hospitable Jewish man. What we liked above all was that we could see the morning sun and the sunset on the Sea of Galilee from our hotel. Seeing the beautiful Galilean sun rising and setting above the lake made my heart feel an unexplainable emotion.

There is a famous food in Galilee. It's Peter's Fish! This flat fish is as big as an adult's palm and grilled. Restaurants with many tourists seemed to all have this dish. But why is it Peter's fish? Is it the fish Peter fished and got a coin out of its mouth? Or is it the fish that his disciples had breakfast in Chapter 21 of the Gospel of John? What did this fish taste like? My curiosity was aroused, but in our budget Peter's fish was too expensive. I thought, *"It must have been caught by the fishermen in the Lake of Galilee anyway, so we'll eat something cheaper. Next time, I'll make sure to eat it."* In this way, I overcame the temptation of Peter's Fish. We instead went to a fish store and bought a big, fresh, and chubby fish of another kind. It was a nice-looking big fish with lots of scales. I made a spicy Korean-style fish soup at the hotel with red pepper powder from the Jerusalem market. How did it taste? It's a freshwater fish. I think I needed water parsley and garland chrysanthemum, but it was good to eat. I think I did a good job of buying red pepper powder~

We took a rental car and went around the Sea of Galilee. There were many famous places. Among them was a church that was established where Jesus had taught his disciples the Beatitudes. It was on a high hill overlooking the Lake of Galilee. I thought, *It would have been great to hear the words of Jesus, in such a beautiful place, seeing the breeze blowing and the lake of Galilee shining in the sun.* Perhaps I must have had a misconception that I can learn something only when I have a hard time! Jesus' teaching seems to go beyond my stereotype, even the place of education.

Driving around the Lake of Galilee about two-thirds, we found one of the tourist attractions in Galilee. Various souvenirs are sold, and there are many places to be baptized in the Lake of Galilee. There was an interesting thing there. Catfish! Since I was born, I've never seen catfish so big. They were chubby catfish the size of an adult's legs and with long beards. Most people who live there did not eat scale-less fish, the catfish were not afraid of humans. They were gathered in groups by the waters where people were being baptized, and they were still there even when people approached them. Those who like Korean catfish spicy soup would be quite tempted.

It was 4-5 days since we had been in Galilee. Joshua, who looked at Facebook, said that James and Priscilla are now in Galilee. Wow!! When my husband sent him a message, the answer came back quickly. We decided to meet by the Sea of Galilee. It was nice to meet the people we met before leaving Korea, and here after DTS. We spent half a day together and talked about this and that. James asked us to come to the United States for our next destination. But at that time, we had already bought a flight ticket to Brazil, so we didn't comment. Anyway, we were all amazed at the miraculous coincidence of meeting James and Priscilla on the shores of the Sea of Galilee in Israel.

The day before we left Israel, before heading to the Tel Aviv Airport, we went to the location where Jesus was baptized that James told us. It was close to the Judean wilderness, on the border with the Jordan River. It was a desert with a little reddish yellow soil. Heavily armed Israeli and Jordanian soldiers were guarding beside the Jordan River. Despite the strict-looking scenery, the Jordan River calmly flows through the desert, and it was a place where we could feel reverence and peace. It was the dry season, so the water was shallow and pretty green. It was on the other side of the airport, it was a long way back down, but it was worthwhile to get there.

During our time in Israel, we spent two weeks in Jerusalem and one week in Galilee for a total of three weeks. The low hills, small olive trees, and the Jordan River seemed smaller than I thought. The landscapes were small and cuter than I had imagined. At first, I was a little disappointed when I saw the simple nature of Israel that felt too small in some way. However, the more I spent time in Israel, the more affection I felt towards it, like a small, cute Asian face you look at often. I was drawn to the country. Jerusalem, where so many Jews live like the stars in the sky. I saw the faithfulness of God, who continues to keep His promise to Abraham for thousands of years. And Jerusalem is a place where I can feel the sovereignty of God, who is in control of history.

But not all good things happened in Israel. As soon as we left the airplane, we were questioned by a security guard. It was probably because of the military-style backpacks we were carrying. I showed my passport for identification, but I was nervous about the unexpected inspection. Perhaps because of ethnic conflicts in Jerusalem, soldiers with guns were guarding everywhere, so I felt little bit anxious.

Nevertheless, why do I miss the place and want to go again? While in Jerusalem, I meditated on Jacob's life. Jacob, who called God his father Isaac's God and not his God due to a painful wound until he was over 100 years old. God waited till the end for Jacob. God protected Jacob whenever he was in trouble and healed his wounds through Joseph. As HE did to Jacob, so HE did to Israel. Like this, God covered my trespasses and was leading me to recovery through His healing grace. I felt the love of the Almighty Lord, who is still faithfully fulfilling His promise given in the Bible. I could feel God's loving gaze more in Israel. So it seems that Israel is a holy land. That's why I miss Israel even now.

The last thing we did in Israel before we left was visiting the Jordan River in the Judean Wilderness where Jesus was baptized. After this, our schedule in Israel was over. The next day we left Israel on an EasyJet to Germany on a bargain sale ticket.

CHAPTER 24

Redirection

When we made plans to go from Sweden to Israel via Europe, we decided to go to Eastern Europe by expanding our faith according to Genesis 13:17, "Go, walk through the length and breadth of the land." Among the Eastern European countries, the Czech Republic was the easiest to travel to at the time. On February 6, we arrived in Berlin, Germany, and caught a bus to the Czech Republic the next morning. We arrived in the capital Prague in the evening after about five hours.

The next day, we wandered around downtown Czech Republic. After passing Eastern European architecture, we crossed the famous bridge with many sculptures on the bridge and entered the old town. There were swans in groups by the river. When I saw the beautiful swans floating in the calm river, I realized, *Ah, I am in Europe.* And I gave them the crumbs I had for breakfast with joy. But too many swans came. Swans were struggling to be the first to eat the bread crumbs. Where did those elegant beings go??!! In front of food, the swans were like ducks. It was a moment when the fantasy of the swan cracked. To me, swans are now long-necked, big ducks. I hurriedly said bye to the swans who had a similar appetite to me and returned from the river to the old castle.

We met David, a YWAM missionary in the Czech Republic, that evening. We had dinner together at the Czech restaurant he had picked. It was like a cafeteria where you picked the food you wanted while passing by with a plate. It was practical, and we could eat the Czech local food. David and his wife said they were expelled for missionary work in another Eastern European country. They stayed in the Czech Republic and were preparing for new pioneer work. As he spoke calmly, I felt that he and his wife had experienced many difficulties in the past and were presently going through some hardships. During our meeting, we decided to worship together at the church they were attending. On Sunday morning, we went to the second floor of a building on a street with many restaurants. What used to be a club on weekdays became a chapel on Sunday. About 40-50 people gathered to worship at the place where the smell of cigarette smoke remained strong. We eagerly praised and hoped that the wind of the Holy Spirit would blow in the Czech Republic and that the church would rise again.

On February 10, we returned to Amsterdam again. We claimed the luggage we had left for a month. In the meantime, we were grateful to the Amsterdam IBIS hotel near the airport, which kept our luggage safe and was clean, cheap, and convenient-for European hotel prices. We were going to catch a flight to Brazil and headed for a transit country. When we prayed about where to go next at the Vilhelmina Base, at the end of December, I had found a Chilean peso coin on the kitchen floor. Then, on the way to Israel, while waiting for the next flight at the Stockholm Airport in Sweden, Joshua found by chance an airline selling tickets to Brazil at a special buy one get one for 1 Euro price. We thought that the place to go after Israel would be South America or Brazil, so we bought a ticket with joy saying, "The Lord blesses the next journey with a special flight ticket." The plane was one way to Brazil.

But the day before we left for the country of transit, Joshua found out that he needed a visa. While he was preparing to travel to Brazil, he only checked my visa. He thought he could enter the country without a visa. But it turns out that for Brazil, Koreans are visa-free, and Americans need a visa. Besides, it takes 1-2 weeks to get a visa for Americans. He called the airline to ask if he could change our flight schedule. The answer was no. All we could do now was ask for intercession. I sent an urgent email to my close friends. On the night of February 11, we departed for the transit country with a heavy heart. We arrived at dawn. We waited until dawn at the airport and planned to apply for a visa at the Brazilian Embassy in the morning. But after praying together, we changed our plans. We decided to stay there and pray more about our next journey, so we went to the guest house we had contacted in advance.

First, we looked back at the cause of this situation. The result was entirely our fault. After asking the Lord about the journey to go after Israel, we did not wait for the Lord's answer. Since we went to Africa and Europe, we assumed the next was South America or Oceania. Then when we saw a cheap flight to Brazil, we even bought a ticket saying "Wow, the next country is Brazil!" We also bought accommodations to stay in Brazil at a bargain price. There were no refunds because it was a special price. About $1,700 disappeared into thin air. Even now, it is a sad experience for me. Realizing this, we repented together to the Lord of our presumption and of acting unwisely.

However, I still have a lot of regrets! It was a waste of money, but I was even more heartbroken because I could not hear the voice of the Lord and had made a mistake. Even then, the Lord of grace comforted me as we worshipped and read the Word. That morning's devotion, which was from Mark 16, was about the women going to the tomb to apply spices that were prepared. The women didn't remember the words of Jesus, and they bought expensive spices that they didn't need. It felt like the women were like us. We didn't hear the voice of the Lord leading us, so we bought a plane ticket that we didn't need in advance. Nevertheless, I was deeply comforted to see the Lord who did not scold the women and instead told the women of the resurrection through his angels. I realized that the Lord, who had accepted those women, would accept me as well. I decided to think more about the grace of the Lord that made me meet good people and that gave us a place to stay safely. And I made up my mind and prayed for our next journey and for the people here.

In fact, ADTS and this vision trip itself were the greatest grace for me. About six months before we got married, I knew the Lord's will concerning my job was, "It's time to leave," so I prayed about my next job. And about a month after we got married, God gave me John 21:6, "Throw your net on the right side of the boat" during the morning devotion time. So I realized that the area where I had been looking for a job the past six months was not where the Lord was leading me. That's when my husband asked me to go to DTS with him. However, I refused with one word because I did not want to live in a community. After my husband spoke to me, I should have prayed and been more attentive. The Lord had given me an answer through my husband, but I did not have ears to hear. After all, the cost of the two years I spent in a place that was not where I was supposed to be was quite a lot. I learned the importance of health after experiencing damage to both retinas of my eyes. The Lord came to me to give me another chance, gave me the heart to do DTS, and opened up the situation to do a DTS. Through this, I came to know the Lord is the One who gives me another chance even if I miss the opportunity of not hearing the Lord's will. Indeed, the grace of the Lord is deep and deeper still.

Valentine's Day on February 14. We left our worries behind that day and decided to go sightseeing. However, on the way to the prayer room in the morning, Joshua and I were hurt by something that we cannot remember now. As we walked along the street, our voices rose, and we argued. And a little later we reconciled as if nothing had happened. And after praying, we went to see the tourist attractions. We had a satisfactory date, and on our way back, we bought a small cake for the couple for providing us with a safe and good place to stay.

I pressed the doorbell. Dingdong~The door opened slightly. "Hello. Today is Valentine's Day... " The wife, who looked at me with an unusual expression, said. "You fought in the morning!" "Huh?! How did you know that??" She said, "I saw everything on the veranda in the morning," and she smiled meaningfully...'*Oh my!!! I got caught. It seems that our voices rang like an echo in the alley early in the morning. Our private conversation in Korean was not so private after all!*' Valentine's Day in 2014 passed like this...

A few days later, we realized it wasn't time to go to Brazil, yet. Instead, we found out that God was leading us to

America, not Brazil. We didn't even think about America. James, whom we had met in Israel, said, "Come to America." I thought, *'We're going to Brazil...'*, so I didn't listen. Yet the Lord must have told me through him at that time. Like Gideon, who wanted to know God's will surely with the fleece, we prayed more. Even so, HE kept giving us the same heart and we started preparing to go to the USA.

There was no direct flight to Kansas City, so we booked a flight to New York. However, it was said that there was a problem with the airfield because it had snowed a lot in the eastern United States. Inevitably, we canceled the flight we had booked and decided to enter through Los Angeles via London. We had to get our plane tickets again and get a US visa-ESTA, but the internet that worked well suddenly had issues. Whatever the cause, we couldn't fix it. We couldn't do anything about the issue. Then my credit card also said that there was a security problem, and the payment suddenly failed. We didn't have a lot of cash, so would we be trapped here?! There were many frustrating things that made us stressed.

Sunday came along. We went to a local church to worship. The pastor read Jeremiah 50. The verses 33-34 impacted me. "This is what the LORD Almighty said. The children of Israel and the descendants of Judah are oppressed together. Those who hold them firmly and refuse to let them go. But their savior is strong. The LORD Almighty is his name." When I heard these words, I was convinced that "a strong God will save us from the interfering spiritual forces and lead us on the path we need to go."

The next day, the second day, the Internet continued to be jammed. We decided to try the internet somewhere other than the guesthouse. We went to the prayer room with our laptops. We tried to connect to the Internet in the lobby. Failed! There was a meeting in the lounge so we could not use it. Someone told us to enter the empty prayer room. We moved and gave it another try. In the midst of nervousness, we suddenly had success! Finally, the Internet was connected!! Hallelujah!! In the room where prayers have been piled up for years, my visas was accepted at once. We quickly tried to buy plane tickets, too. But the internet was blocked again. Still, I was very happy to get a visa within the 5-minute window. People who heard the good news rejoiced with us when we informed them of the news that the visa was resolved.

One of the people told us to get a flight ticket through a travel agency. She knew our credit card had a problem, so she tried to lend her own. Looking at the people who were willing to help strangers in need, even though they don't know us well, I felt the Korean affection and Christian kindness. But we couldn't accept her kind offer because it would have been too much. We decided to try a little more to get the plane ticket. We walked the streets and tried to withdraw cash from ATM machines at every bank we saw. But it failed several times. How many times had it been... It seemed to be around the whole area. My leg hurt, and the deadline set by the travel agency to purchase the reserved tickets was approaching. There seemed to be no more banks. The moment I was about to give up, there was another ATM machine in the corner. We ran there. Will it work this time? With a little hope, I put the card in. A tense moment!! Soon, I heard the sound of the machine counting out the money. Finally, the withdrawal was successful!! There was not much time left. We ran and bought a plane ticket out of the country from the travel agency. So, a thrilling 7 nights and 8 days passed in the transit country. We said goodbye to the thankful guest house people for accepting us. And we went to the airport.

CHAPTER 25

London Eye

February 19. We arrived at London Gatwick Airport. We took the airport shuttle bus to London Heathrow to buy a flight ticket to Los Angeles. There were only 7 seats left. Thank you, God! I received a ticket, but there was more to it besides the boarding pass. Looking at it closely, I saw that it was a ticket to the London Eye!! It was an airline event. Ha ha!! We had time to tour London for half an afternoon, but since we were on a budget, we couldn't afford to go sightseeing and ride the London Eye. But it became possible~ The weather helped, too. It is said that the river Thames did not overflow because the heavy rain stopped the night before.

The London Eye, which used to come out often when watching movies in Korea! I prayed to the Lord that I wanted to visit there once every time I saw it on the big screen, but I didn't expect Him to fulfill my prayers like this! We saw Big Ben, took a picture in front of my husband's favorite Churchill statue, and went to the London Eye. London, which I saw when the ferris wheel climbed the highest, was a huge city with no end! There was also a bonus from the Lord on the walk back to the airport. I turned around and looked across the Thames River and saw the London Eye once more. The white London Eye was dyed orange in the sunset. We stopped to see the beautiful scenery that could not be captured with a camera and watched the orange-colored London Eye for a while. It was a grateful experience when I felt with my heart that the Father grants his daughter's wishes.

The next day, we went to the airport by the first bus. Our departure time was 11 o'clock, and there were still hours left. As tiredness came all at once, my nerves became sensitive. At that time, my husband told me about what happened in the evening two days ago. At the airport of the transit country, he was thinking about the route of travel in England. When he prayed about what to do, the Lord said, "Take a bus instead of the subway when you go to Heathrow Airport, even if it is more expensive, so that Heejin can enjoy London." When he obeyed and bought a bus ticket, he got a £20 discount. The Lord even told my husband who was praying to take the bus for me who had wanted to see London! And the Lord made it possible for my husband to get a discount on bus tickets too so that he wasn't stressed out! HE is the Lord who pays attention to details. The complaints that had risen in my heart disappeared, and gratitude flowed out. I thanked the Lord and thanked my husband for obeying the Lord. I was happy in London because of the beautiful London Eye, a joyful London afternoon, and above all, the Lord who gave me precious memories. It was time to board. We left London behind and boarded a flight to Los Angeles.

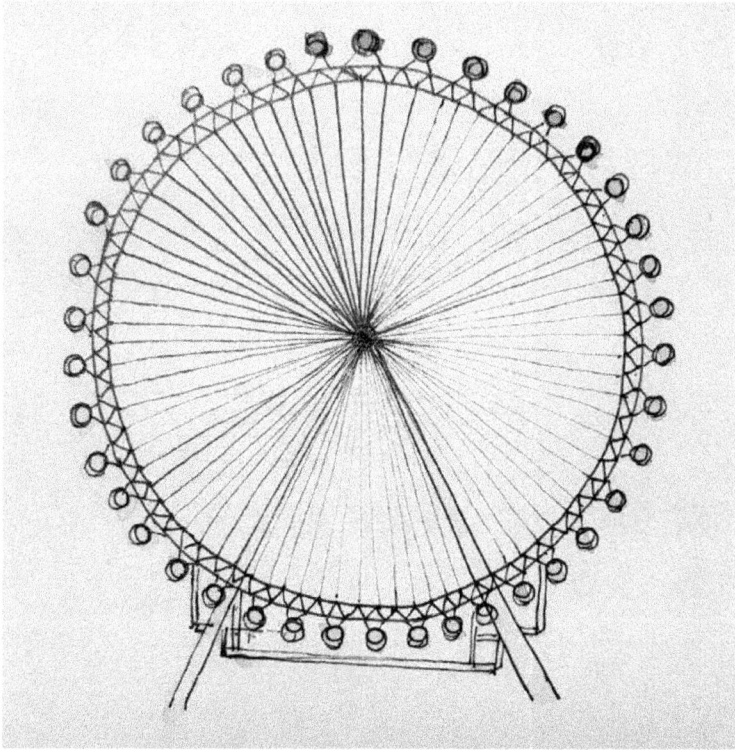

Fig 9. London Eye

PART V. THE LONG COURSE

From London, UK via LA, USA
To Kansas City

CHAPTER 26

Kansas City, USA

We arrived in Kansas City on February 21 via Los Angeles. The next day, we met Jinyoung. She is my friend who had been in the same study group when I was studying the Bible at the church Bible school in Korea. We had studied the Pentateuch and the Old Testament together for a year. She asked us to stay at her place until we could find a place to stay. She stayed in the dormitory of the bible college that she attended. It was a small, bright, and clean place with a room, living room, kitchen, and bathroom. My husband and I decided to stay in the living room. H, who lived downstairs, heard about us and lent us an electric mat so we could sleep warmly.

But why did the Lord lead us to America? America was where my husband grew up, so it was totally out of our main journey guidelines. I didn't know why we had come here yet. However, in the process of revising the direction of our journey in the transit country, there were words that had caught my eye when I was doing Quiet Time. By combining those verses, we thought that the reason He called us to the next step was to have fellowship with Jesus and to give us a mission. And while I was in America, I was hoping that maybe the Lord would give us a baby we had been waiting for. So, unlike the journey so far, I thought that we could be in the U.S. for a long time.

With Jinyoung's help, we rented a small apartment near the Prayer House in a few days. We moved in March 1st. The move was very simple since we only had two bags and two backpacks. She took us to the house of Deacon K, who was having an indoor yard sale since she was going to move. The deacon was planning to move to Los Angeles after spending a year praying at the Prayer House. We bought a table and a blanket. The deacon also gave us dishes for free. Looking around at the objects, I saw a small Jewish temple lamp model with seven side branches. I had wanted to buy it in Israel. However, I had hesitated because of the burden of increasing my luggage, so I didn't buy it after all. But Deacon K willingly gave it to me, saying, "Take that too." Through the deacon, I could feel the tender Lord who takes care of even the smallest wants I had forgotten. Even now, the lamp stand is at our house, next to a small cross. With their help, we had a house and household items in an instant. Thank you, Jinyoung and Deacon K!

On our 3rd wedding anniversary, My husband bought a special sale ticket with Groupon. We borrowed James's car and went to a French restaurant near downtown. The tables were full. The meal voucher my husband bought was a set of main dish, salad, and drinks. The person taking the order smiled and gave added soup for the two of us to have as a service. Thanks to her kindness, we were able to eat until we were full. My husband wanted to buy me a present as well, but I refused. Our finances were really tight. Nevertheless, I thanked my husband for remembering and taking care of the anniversary. Even when I think about that day now, seeing that I am still grateful to my husband, I think I was very moved by him that day.

In fact, my body were pretty tired at that time. While in

Europe, I continued to suffer from an unknown cause of gastroenteritis. After about two months, I knew that tap water was the cause, so I bought bottled water and drank it. Only then did diarrhea stop. In addition, it seemed that the tight schedule during that time had been too much for my body. Eventually, I started to have severe hair loss in the United States. I was afraid of what would happen when my hair fell out like this. I prayed earnestly as I looked at the remaining hair that had been drastically reduced. The words of the Lord that He counts all the hairs on our head (Matthew 10:30) were really comforting. I definitely experienced the same hair loss that I had seen when I was studying medicine. The hair that had been missing for several months is now all recovered several years later. Sometimes I hear that I have a lot of hair. Thank you very much, Lord!!

Our schedule revolved around the prayer room - after breakfast, a prayer room, lunch and a prayer room. Two weeks went by like that. I had an unusual dream on the night of March 16. I was running on a playground track with heavy rain. As I went, there was a short track, so I was about to enter there, but I heard a voice from the back, from heaven's direction, saying, "It's not there; it's a longer track." So I went on a longer track and kept running in the rain. *What does this mean?* I didn't know, but I wrote it down in my diary, thinking it was an unusual dream.

On March 18, I bought radish at a grocery store and made Kkakdugi (Korean Kimchi made of small radish in square shape). It was the first kimchi I made after marriage. The taste was not good when I think about it now, but it was delicious back then. It was my first time living in the United States, so there were a few interesting things. First, the electric range in the kitchen! It was a gas stove in Korea and South Africa. Turn it and turn it on, and a blue flame will come out. But here, the thick wire is rolled up and there is no flame. When turned on, the wire turns red and hot. At first, I was curious how to cook with this. But it works well, haha. Secondly, Trader Joe's! Wouldn't it be nice to have a store like this in Korea? It's not big, but there are products from all over the world, and the price is good. If you fry vegetables in olive oil and season with salt, the taste is excellent even if you don't add anything else. Trader Joe's was one of my pleasures in an unfamiliar America~

◆ **Letter to Dream team and Friends - March 2, 2014**

Since the last news, 40 days have passed. It's still a little cold. Yet the long winter is almost over, and I can feel spring already coming~

We are in Kansas City, USA, after our visit to Israel, and after a week in transit country… In the meantime, a lot of changes have happened. Now we are praying and relaxing at the Prayer House Kansas City to help our bodies and minds from the journey that has been fast and has left us breathless.

From the time we left Korea, we have been to 17 countries in 9 months, from a short day to six months, from Africa to Europe and the Middle East, including stopovers. We are grateful to God who has led us to see and learn so many things. And while moving from place to place, there were many things that happened. I would like to give thanks and praise, remembering that all things have been prosperous with the grace of God and your intercession.

We ask for intercession during the time we will spend here in the United States so that we can obey in the Holy Spirit while holding on to Genesis 13:14-18 to travel east, west, north and south. Thank you. I wish you good health during the change of seasons and hope that you will enjoy the warm spring full of the peace and joy of the Lord.

Joshua & Heejin in Kansas City, USA

CHAPTER 27

Plan A Instead of Plan B

My husband and I were having a special Daniel fast together. Our finances were running out, and we had an unresolved financial problem left behind in Korea. While attending DTS and Vision Trip, I thought this issue would be resolved in time, but it hadn't been taken care of. My husband and I were thinking about it and asked James and Priscilla for advice. We went to their home and they heard our situation. James advised, "Don't ignore God's Law of Nature. In order to do this, you must return to Korea." Priscilla also said. "It is more important to know the vision that God gave you than to solve the current problem itself." My husband also said that unless there is a miracle, it would be right to go back to Korea. *'I have to go back to South Korea?! But I don't want to go now…'*

I felt heavy and restless. My family's debts which I was responsible for as the eldest daughter, giving up my dream as a professor and choosing the life of a clinical doctor…I had such bitter wounds due to the life that I had to live, regardless of whether I wanted to or not. Even though I would have a big problem in a few months if I didn't return to Korea and pay off this debt (almost all of it was gone by then, but there was still some left), I was trying my best to ignore this fact. I was buried in painful memories rather than happy memories of my home country. Because it was so difficult, I tried to avoid the unpleasant past. So I really hated going back to Korea.

The next day was March 22. I was praying earnestly for a

miracle to happen in the big prayer room. "If that is solved, there is no problem and everything will work. Lord!!!"' I was crying and praying for a long time. But then, a soft voice was felt. "I love you. My jewel, my jewel, my jewel (I heard 'my jewel' in English)... love yourself as I love you," I heard the voice say quietly. My tears stopped flowing. "Huh? What's the voice I just heard?? Who said this??" I tried to discern. Was it from me? Was it Satan's temptation? Or was it the voice of the Lord? *"Well... I don't think I said "love yourself" because I didn't like myself, and Satan wouldn't say love. Then was it the voice of the Lord?!"* I prayed that the Lord would solve my problem... But the Lord said, "I love you," to me. How much I had wanted to hear Him say this! Moreover, the Lord called me a jewel!! But I wasn't so thrilled back then. It is very embarrassing, but in fact, I would have been more delighted if HE had said at the time, "I will solve it."

Two days later, I was still praying hard for a miracle of the Lord. "God! I don't think I've ever cried for anything in my life for days like this. Please fill our need miraculously. You are Almighty! I want you to listen to me. The daughter you love is petitioning you like this." Sometimes the child acts like a fox. Just as apples fall from an apple tree due to the law of gravity, there are laws made by the Lord that apply in our lives, but I wanted to break them in the name of a miracle. Anyway, at that time, I was really throwing a temper tantrum in front of the Lord. It was the first time in my life. Trust me... While I was crying and praying, I felt a quiet voice! "Write down what you need." My tears stopped flowing. "Yes! finally!" I omitted the process of discernment and quickly pulled out paper and wrote down a list of what I wanted. At this moment, I am looking at the list from 1 to 7 posted in the diary. However, I finally got a response, but in a corner of my heart, I felt uncomfortable.

On March 27, I had quiet time in the morning, and I could see the words that were not seen until now. Philippians 1:21-24 "For to me, to live is Christ and to die is gain. If I am to go on living in the body, this will mean fruitful labor for me. Yet what shall I choose? I do not know! I am torn between the two: I desire to depart and be with Christ, which is better by far; but it is more necessary for you that I remain in the body." It may sound strange, but at that time I understood this verse to mean that the Apostle Paul wanted to be martyred, but he chose the latter because it would be more beneficial to live longer for the church's sake. Looking at these words, I thought, *Is there a choice in this? Is there an option?? Did the Lord give the Apostle Paul a choice?!"* That day my quiet time went like this.

That afternoon I also went to the prayer room. As I prayed while listening to the praise, I remembered a verse. "If one grain of wheat falls to the ground and does not die..." I found the text and read it. John 12:24-27. "Very truly I tell you, unless a kernel of wheat falls to the ground and dies, it remains only a single seed. But if it dies, it produces many seeds. Anyone who loves their life will lose it...Whoever serves me must follow me; and where I am, my servant also will be. Now my soul is troubled, and what shall I say? No, it was for this very reason I came to this hour." When I read these verses, I realized what Jesus wanted to tell me. For me, there are things I want to do now, where I want to be, but going where Jesus wants me to go is serving Him. But in fact, that's good for me, too.

Sacrifice comes at a price, but the result is much fruit. But Jesus also suffered before the cross. Just as I was suffering in front of the problem of going to Korea now... It felt like the Lord understood my distress.

The Lord told me His will, but He also said, "Write down what you need." And like the words of the Bible I read in the morning, the Lord seemed to have given me a choice. As if the Lord said, "Heejin, I think it's best for you to return to Korea. However, if you really want to study in the United States, I will respect your will and give permission." The Lord is the One who can command His will of course, but it seemed that He was not doing so. He instead gave me the example of Jesus and the apostle Paul, and He gave me a choice. My heart was softened by His gentleness, he did not force me. I have lived in a culture where there are many obligations that I have to do. To give me, a choice is to respect me. That was love to me. Since the Lord respected me this way, I wanted to follow the will of the Lord, even if it wasn't what I wanted. I wanted to follow Him because I knew that the choice of the all-knowing and omnipotent Lord is always the best. Even though I don't know now, if I look back later, I will know it was the best. So I chose the will of the Lord even though I didn't really want to. It was back to Korea to live our daily life again following the Lord's laws of nature.

That afternoon, I told my husband about these steps, who had been waiting by my side in silence. 1. When I was running in my dreams, I heard a voice saying, "Go around the long course, not the short course." 2. James's advice to not ignore God's laws of nature. 3. The Bible passage from QT in which Paul makes a choice for the benefit of the church and not the way he wants. 4. The words of John 8:24-27 that came to mind in the afternoon prayer room.

So I came to the conclusion that even if I didn't want to, it was right to go back to Korea. Then I remembered praying, "Lord, let me choose Isaac, not Ishmael." I have prayed to God in this way for the past few years after seeing the trouble in Abraham's family, which was caused by trying to fulfill the Lord's promise by himself with his human thinking. Then I thought that my desire to stay in America to study and not return to Korea might be my timing and not the Lord's timing. If so, it was not Plan A but Plan B, and I would have to deal with the bad consequences that would arise. Thinking like this, I was able to surrender my desire to study in the U.S.A.

A while later, I had a unique dream that I still remember clearly. In my dream, I was walking energetically on a bumpy dirt road, and a lion was lying down in front of the road. However, I wasn't afraid and lifted the lion with one hand, broke its jaw, and threw it away. It was an unimaginable dream for me, who was timid and usually hated being alone in a dark house. Thinking about that dream still cheers me up. I felt like the Lord was encouraging me to overcome the lion which represented fear so that I would live inside of the Lord's will. Perhaps laying down what I wanted to do and obeying the timing of the Lord was the climax of the DTS and the journey that followed.

To be honest, I could see through this process that the Lord did His best to kindly inform me of His will. But that wasn't the only thing. The Lord called me His jewel. At that time, I didn't know the significance of this phrase, but

I was happy and felt good to hear HIM call me that. But it was really important between God and me. My name is Heejin. It is a name made from Chinese characters which mean "to shine " and "to be true," respectively. My parents gave me this name to mean "to be truly shining".

Actually, I wondered why God called me His jewel. My curiosity grew bigger and bigger, but I couldn't figure it out. But I found out recently while editing this (Seven years after hearing God's voice while praying at the Prayer House in 2014). The Lord had called me by my name's meaning. The Lord told me that when I receive the light of the Lord, I am the jewel of the Lord that reflects beautiful twinkling light. I think of myself as a stone that is nothing, but to the Lord, I am a precious stone. To be honest, I still can't quite believe it. I think I need to be healed of how I view myself. At that time, I think the Lord wanted to show me what kind of existence I am to Him. It's like saying, "You are precious to me," to your beloved child.

Anyway, what would the result be if I didn't choose the Lord's will because my desire was greater at that time? Perhaps a person with bad credit??!! Looking back now, I think, "Whew! What a close call!" Medical missionary dream team friends, husband, and DTS... The love of the Lord I received through them...The tender and delicate love of the Lord accumulated in my heart, and I was able to discern the Lord's will. I was able to face the wounds of the past and choose to return to Korea in obedience to the Lord.

As Psalm 138:3 says, "When I called, you answered me; you greatly emboldened me." I am deeply grateful to the Lord for guiding me with His love. The Lord, the Shepherd who has led my life until now, will continue to guide me faithfully by His love and grace. "The LORD is my shepherd, I shall not be in want."

Fig 10. He is my good shepherd :)

CHAPTER 28

Community Prayer and Fasting in Unity

On April 7, the Korean leader James suggested that the leaders of each country fast and pray together for a week. It touched our hearts to pray together in unity and to rely on the Lord to breakthrough the problems we were facing. Thus, we decided to join this fast for unity and breakthrough and to go deeper. I had to do it for seven days, but to my shame, I had never done a water only fast. While my husband was fasting, I couldn't eat alone. So I decided to do it for 3 days. I started water only fasting for the first time in my life. At first, I was gloomy about the fasting because I could only have water. But there was grace. Surprisingly, I was less hungry. Drinking warm water little by little, I relieved my cold and hunger(As a doctor - please check with your physician before fasting). As I escaped from my routine kitchen life, I also experienced freedom from what to eat. And 3 days, which seems to be very long, passed faster than expected~

To talk more about fasting, the Lord gave me great grace every time I fasted. Perhaps because he is a compassionate God, He has pity on me who is not good at fasting. The first fast I had was straw fast! You may have guessed what it is, but to explain, it's fasting to eat something you can eat with a straw. While attending medical missions, the grace accumulated more and more, and one day in 2007, I wanted to completely quit drinking alcohol. Like many Korean dramas, the relationship between seniors and juniors is strict in the medical world. I wanted to end my drinking life, but it was still difficult at my new job after leaving the university hospital. My senior, who is the head of the workplace, also liked alcohol. The hospital run by the senior worked on every Sunday and holiday except Chuseok (Lunar Thanksgiving Day) and Lunar New Year's Day. I said I was a Christian at the interview. And my boss, the hospital owner, very reluctantly agreed for me to work on all public holidays for not working on Sundays. However, he did not give up alcohol.

A year passed. Ahead of the company dinner in March, I felt an intense desire to quit drinking, so I decided to cling to the Lord and fast. However, even though I decided to fast for the first time in my life, I was so hungry. And I didn't want to interfere with my work. Thus, it was straw fasting that I thought up and I thought it was reasonable following the cry in my stomach. So I had only milk and juice for 3 days. My own prayers with weak faith felt insufficient. So I did one more thing. On my church intercession card, I wrote down my desperate desire to quit drinking. I believed the intercessory prayer team would help me in prayer.

Finally, D-Day, March 31, 2007, dinner meeting with the doctors and my boss. At the first meal, I could pretend to drink. But there was a second round on that day. We had to sit in a circle and, one by one, drink from our glass. And now it has become unavoidable. Holding onto my trembling heart, I took courage and said in a small voice that I wanted to stop drinking to the boss who was next to me. He thinks for a moment, "Really?! Then I'll drink it for you!" he declared as he lifted my glass and gulped it down. It was a miracle! After that day, my senior no longer tried to force me to drink during company dinners, and I could officially quit drinking. Hallelujah!! This is how the LORD answered for the prayers of the intercessory prayer teams, and to my insufficient straw fasting.

This time, too, the Lord faithfully answered our fasting prayers. During the Community United Fast, God helped the two of us to reflect on our lives. Looking back over our past years, we had a lot to repent of. We had poorly managed our time, talents, health, and finances. I realized that I was an unfaithful steward who had mismanaged what the Lord gave me. We were united in repentance to the Lord. And we prayed earnestly for the Lord's help as we decided to fix the collapsed areas in our lives when we returned to Korea again.

The night before departing for Korea as the night was getting deeper, I couldn't sleep. It was because of the burden of having to face the difficult past again in the present. However, I didn't want to turn the beliefs I had learned through the DTS and the subsequent vision trip into just one good memory. As Philip taught during the 10th week of the lecture, I had to be brave like Joshua and the Israelite soldiers who fought fiercely with the five kings to occupy the Promised Land. *"Okay! Let's have courage and rely on the Lord who loves me! Let's go!!"* In this way, I put aside the pressure that was holding my heart. And that night, I sent an email to my brother, friends, and the Dream Team~

◆ Letter to Daehui (my dear younger brother), Dream team, and Friends - April 18, 2014

Hello~ It's already been two months since we arrived here. When I first came, there were only dry branches, and the grass was still yellow. However, two weeks ago, new light green leaves appeared on the trees, flowers such as dandelion, forsythia, and magnolia bloomed, and birds have been busy preparing to lay eggs. Yesterday I saw two new little bird nests on the "R" and "S" of a signboard at a restaurant, and they were really cute haha~

With the Korean Community as the main axis, international leaders here had a joint fasting prayer together, and Joshua and I also joined. I thanked God for the abundant testimonies of the individuals and communities in attendance. Joshua and I also had great grace from God. Before I started fasting this time, I had a dream, and it was a dream where the two of us were bathing in a large bucket in a big classroom. Moreover, after a few days of fasting, we began to repent, too, and both Joshua and I cried a lot.

While we prayed, I accepted the crucifixion of Jesus more deeply into my heart. Since I was young, I couldn't feel the love that Jesus showed through the cross. It was weird. Then there was a realization of myself, of Jesus, and of the cross. When I prayed this time, I remembered the words about forgiveness in Matthew 18, while dealing with the subject of forgiveness. I realized that I had no awareness of being a sinner who had been forgiven of 10,000 talents. Realizing that, I prayed and asked the Holy Spirit to remove the veil from my eyes.

The next day, while I was organizing my diary, I realized that instead of Jesus, I was in the center of my heart. On the outside, it looks like Jesus is the center of my heart, but like a yolk in an egg white, I was deeper in the middle. I thought about how this could be and looked deeply into my heart. There was a deep sense of shame and inferiority in the center that thought of myself as having problems. And at the same time, I had strong self-awareness and pride which were like two sides of a coin. And I realized that I was reliant on self-righteousness, not Jesus' righteousness. I had a self-centered relationship with Jesus.

Realizing this, I knew that I had crucified Jesus like the Pharisees of that time. And even though Jesus knew all this about my heart, I realized that Jesus forgave me and interceded with the Heavenly Father to forgive me because I didn't know what I was doing. I deeply felt the love of Jesus, who loved me until His death, not with my head but with my heart. I thanked the Heavenly Father for giving me His only Son and Jesus for giving me Himself. And I repented of the idolatry of serving myself. After repenting of my transgressions and sins which God showed in His love, I am glad that I have become closer to God.

Joshua, who wept next to me during prayer time, also regained his calling as a pastor. Through this fasting prayer, I thank the Lord for removing the wall of my heart that was blocking my relationship with God. I haven't felt a big change yet, but I declare that the gospel of the cross that was planted in my heart like a mustard seed has already sprung up in my life. Hallelujah!! On a spring day when the flowers are in full bloom, Joshua and I went back after prayer time and shared with one another what we had repented of haha~

And one important news is that our next stop is the motherland!!!! As in the journey so far, I feel the mystery of God's providence once again as I see God's timing and guidance beyond our thoughts. At first I thought, *Then is this missionary trip over now?!* But I found out that our journey with God continues, even though it looks different.

And I asked God what this trip means to me. Through this trip, I realized how much my values and life were tainted by the world and repented of this. If the departure 11 months ago was the exodus from those worldly values, then I learned that this return is to enter Canaan, the land of promise.

I am glad and thankful that I can hear the voices of my loved ones and see their faces again, and leave all my worries to the LORD. And...Tteokbokki (spicy rice cake dish), Black Bean Noodles Jajangmyeon, Korean Beef Soup Rice, sweet and sour pork, Budaejjigae (spam and sausage kimchi stew - After the Korean War, Koreans used the spam and sausage from the American army and added it to their kimchi stew.)...*I've been fine, but...How was I able to fast?*" This sudden, strong attraction for food! Meal appointments are welcome! Save your pocket money! Hahaha!! Korea, wait for us! I'll see you soon on one of these blooming spring days.

Joshua & Heejin from Kansas City

CHAPTER 29

Coming back to South Korea

Joshua and I decided to return to Korea via Portland, Oregon. Until then, after our marriage, I had not yet met my sister-in-law. On April 18, they met us at the airport. Sister-in-law and I met for the first time, but it wasn't awkward since we were similar to each other. My face resembles my husband a lot. When people see us, they often think that we are siblings. When my sister-in-law and the two of us are side by side, we look like three siblings. She carefully cooked ribs for us even though she wasn't feeling well. I was grateful to my sister-in-law. We spent four days and three nights together and had a worship service on Easter Sunday. The next day, early in the morning, on April 21, we flew to Seoul.

On April 22, we arrived in Seoul. We took the airport bus and got off near the neighborhood where our friend Joseph and his wife lived. When we opened the door to his house, two cute girls welcomed us. They were Joseph's daughters, aged 7 and 4, who resemble their father and mother. Casablanca was also there. I was so happy to see them! I was encouraged by my friends' hospitality. We lived in community with Joseph's family for 100 days from that day on. Actually, we came back a few years earlier to Korea than we had planned, so we had nowhere to go. Yet they welcomed us and gave us a place to stay. I thank the Lord for giving us a generous family friend filled with faith, even when they didn't have enough themselves, and a place where we can live!

We went to reconnect the cell phone. But how fast the staff spoke... I had a hard time understanding what he was saying.. There were so many buses and cars. Seoul, a huge city that moves so busily. It felt like Seoul, where I was, wasn't real, and I felt like a stranger. *"It's been less than a year since I left our country. What's wrong with me? It wasn't like this when I went to outreach after taking a lecture in South Africa, so why is it more difficult in Korea? What am I doing wrong?"* To me, who was so confused, my husband explained that it was a culture shock that I felt when I returned to my hometown. My husband must have struggled, too, but next to me, "It's okay. It's normal," he said, and I was relieved. Then I remembered it. It was the emotional confusion that I learned in the DTS class, which can happen if I go home after training. It may be different for each person, but in my case, it was harder when I came back home than when I went to a new place. Thanks to the Instructor and Victor for letting me know about this during the debriefing session. Fortunately, after about a month, I started getting better.

Sunday arrived. I attended a Sunday worship service in Korea. When I sang a song in Korean in a familiar chapel, I realized that I had come back to my hometown. The theme of the sermon on that day was "twelve baskets left after the miracle of five fish and two bread" The pastor explained why Jesus had the disciples gather the leftovers after performing the miracle. As I listened to the sermon, I checked my own condition. And I could understand more why the Lord brought me back to Korea. After completing the DTS missionary training, I could fall into spiritual pride because of my special experiences in the mission field. Like James and John, the sons of thunder who said,

"Shall we pray for fire from heaven?" (Luke 9:54). I realized that HE had made me come to my original place so that I could not fall into this trap and digest what I learned in reality. It wasn't my desire, so I was full of uncomfortable feelings, but listening to the sermon that day made me feel comfortable. Thank You, Lord, for having me reflect on my spiritual state once again.

While at a friend's house, we started small group meetings again. Joseph and his wife, Benjamin' family, and Joshua and I. Benjamin' family also returned from DTS in Jeju Island. It was a cell group family reunion! During the past year, all three families had been training in spiritual places where the Lord lead them. And we gathered again in the name of 'Wednesday Prayer Meeting'. We encouraged and comforted each other by sharing the Lord's grace to each of us and the various things we experienced. It was an unstable time with a slight fear of the unknown future and a time for all three families to start anew. However, just gathering together every Wednesday to cook and talk to each other was a great help.

My husband and I decided to fight the 5 kings in our lives to claim the promised land, as we learned in the 10th week of the DTS class. The Lord has revealed the targets we must fight at times through the Community United Fasting and Prayer Meeting. Now it was time to practice in our lives what we had repented of with tears! Mismanaged time, talents, health, finances... We began to rebuild where we had fallen and weakened. But… it wasn't easy. I really had to push myself. I did QT every day and tried to hear the voice of the Lord. The Lord who came as my God in Cambodia, and the Lord who worked strongly in South

Africa! I engraved in my heart that HE would still lead my life in Korea.

First, to maintain our health, we started stretching as Philip taught us in his lecture. Joseph's family was also with us. We got together in a circle with Joseph, his wife, and his two children to stretch together every day. We also started to rebuild the walls of financial stewardship in our lives. For me, who didn't have a concept of money, it was a big deal to write a household account book to record income and expenditures. The Lord gave me an example and encouraged me. At the time, my friend, Joseph's wife, listened to the King's Finances Lecture by Missionary Mijin Kim and was practicing it (The King's Finances is a testimony of her application of Christian financial principles, which were found in *Wealth, Riches and Money; God's Biblical Principles of Finance* [Crag Hill & Earl Pitts, published by YWAM], in her life). My friend applied it to empty the refrigerator! She cooked the old kimchi in the kimchi refrigerator in many different ways. Old kimchi tastes good in any dish. Thanks to my friend, I also learned to empty the refrigerator. In this way, the Lord helped us put into practice the Christian financial principles we learned in Victor's lectures in South Africa by giving us a companion to help us.

◆ **Letter to Dream team and Friends - End of June 2014**

Hello? We have sent you greetings after a long time. It's already been two and a half months since I wrote the last letter~ I wonder how you all are doing these days.

We returned to Seoul after the last newsletter. It rains

often because it is the rainy season in Seoul right now. All the places I went to for the past 11 months were in winter, so it seemed a little hot when I came to Korea. I returned to Korea sooner than expected, so there was nowhere to go until we had a home of our own. Thankfully, our friends, who were intercessors, opened their home and welcomed us.

I wanted to say hello to my friends and family after I arrived, and there were many things to do. However, when I came back, the jet lag and the fatigue that had accumulated over the year came over me and I was so tired that I spent the first few weeks like a hibernating bear.

With the loving intercession and deep consideration of our friends, with a comfortable bed and delicious food, with a warm welcome from my dear friends and Dream Team members, and with Wednesday's prayer group that God gathered together again, I've been relieved of all my physical and mental fatigue due to traveling during the past year. Hallelujah~Thank God!! Thank you so much to my friend's and family!

From Joshua and Heejin in Seoul

CHAPTER 30

Vision Trip

After several weeks of rest, I started to attend an early morning service at a church near my friend's house. During early morning service, the pastor began preaching from the Gospel of Matthew about the Kingdom of Heaven. Every day that we heard the word about the kingdom of heaven, our hearts were excited again and we were energized. My husband had been looking forward to a great revival since he was young. As for me, his wife? To be honest, I wasn't really interested. It was just fun to listen to when my husband talked passionately. But then, through DTS and missionary trips, I had a passionate heart for missionary work, and I listened to my husband's story about the coming Great Revival. It was an amazing change.

Anyway we returned to Korea, but we did not know where to go or what to do in the future. My husband and I seriously thought about these things. First, we wanted to hear where the will of the Lord was for us. Joshua and I had a special Daniel fast for 7 days, seeking the grace of the Lord. After the Sunday service on July 13, we met Elder Lee, one of the Dream Team leaders and someone who interceded for us, at the church. After listening to our story, Elder Lee advised us to ask God for confirmation like Gideon while doing a vision trip. So, we decided to go on a vision trip to see where the promised land was to be given to us, just as in Joshua 18. *"Where should we go?"* There was a place where my husband wanted to go. When my husband ministered at a church in Korea about 11 years ago, he went on a summer mission and was very impressed when he went to Jindo, Jeollanam-do (an island in the southwest of Korea, this is where our famous Jindo dogs came from). Thus, we decided to go on a vision trip to Jeollanam-do.

On July 24, Joshua and I took a train and departed for Jeollanam-do, each carrying a backpack, just like we did during our trip to Israel. The first place I visited in Jeollanam-do was Yeosu, where I had happy memories of my childhood. Upon arrival, we went to the church I went to during middle school. We went to the church office and shared that we were there on a vision trip. The office staff welcomed us (even though we were unfamiliar visitors), and the senior pastor opened the missionary quarters.

The next morning, while looking around the missionary guest house, I saw pictures of past pastors hanging on the wall. Yeosu First Presbyterian Church was a church with more than 100 years of history, and there were pictures of the first all to the way to the current, 13th, pastor. Looking at the pictures, I found a familiar face that I seemed to have seen before. Looking at the name written below, it was the same as my maternal great-grandfather's name. When I took a picture and checked with my mother and my youngest aunt, I found out that he was the same person. My family came to know, for the first time, that he had served at this church for two years. When I spoke to the senior pastor, he was very happy that the fourth pastor's great-granddaughter had come. Senior Pastor Seongcheon Kim, who loves history, records the church's 100-year past and present, and is recovering the local Christian history. Thanks to him, I learned about my maternal great-grandfather.

By the grace of God, we had a pleasant relationship in Yeosu for a few days, and then left for Mokpo for our next destination. Choi, who is the director of YWAM Mokpo, welcomed us on the next stop of our Vision Trip. She talked with us and told us that the Mokpo area is one of the key places for the Korean church and missionary work. While talking about various things, the conversation led to Hebron Hospital in Cambodia, and it turned out that director Choi and Missionary Lee, the vice president of Hebron Hospital, had a close relationship. At that time, a call came to her, and it was Missionary Lee who came to Korea for a visit. We were all amazed by the connection that the Lord connected to each other, and we spent time with the director until evening. After staying overnight at YWAM Mokpo, we headed to Gwangju. At that time, there was a special summer seminar for youth hosted by YWAM Gwangju, so we attended. There, we met Missionary Lee and his wife. The missionaries listened to Joshua and me, shared their stories, and encouraged us. After completing the Jeollanam-do Vision Trip, we returned to our friend's house in Seoul.

Through the Jeollanam-do Vision Trip, my husband and I met good people, and through this, we felt the grace and providence of the Lord greatly. We thought, *"Among the places we visited in Jeollanam-do, wouldn't the Yeosu and Suncheon area be the place the Lord opens up?"* With a heart for missions and preparing for revival, we wanted to build a missions center there. But considering our situation, it seemed impossible, and I was afraid. Still, I didn't want to waste what I had learned through the DTS and subsequent mission trips over the past 11 months. *"So we don't have a house or finances right now and are afraid, but like other missionaries, should we overcome our fear and jump with faith first?"* My husband and I thought. We took action right away. We went to Yeosu to find a house to rent and then came to Seoul to pack our luggage. We also needed a car because we were going to a province where the transportation wasn't as extensive as in Seoul. However, we couldn't afford to buy a car because the money we had saved had been exhausted. We prayed to the Lord for our needs. A few days later, my cousin gladly gave me the car he was using, saying that he was planning to buy a new car. This is how we have our own Dongulee (This is our car's nickname; it means "round".) In the small micro-car, we packed the kitchenware that our friend had prepared for us, and we packed our blankets and left for Yeosu on August 8 with our friend couple to send us off.

Beautiful Yeosu with bright sunshine and pretty islands. We unpacked our luggage and had fun going around the neighborhood. Here we decided to wait for God's guidance and the doors to open. And we went to the early morning service at Yeosu First Presbyterian Church near our house. After a week, the senior pastor (who met Joshua and me during the Vision Trip) and his wife seemed surprised. The reason was probably because we were very daring. However, the pastor and wife quietly served us by meeting with us whenever they had time and buying us some delicious food.

Our health improved more and more. Goso-dong, where our house was, was made from a small mountain in front of the sea. Wherever we went, we had to go uphill and downhill. In the small and pretty city of Yeosu, we walked as much as possible. Bright sunlight, warm sea breeze, hillside road and early morning worship created an environment in which I couldn't help but become healthy. And fresh seafood!! Yeosu has a lot of crab dishes such as crab pickled in soy sauce and blue crab doenjang (Korea soybean paste) soup. Yum~Just thinking about these foods makes me drool~~ Joshua and I like to eat inexpensive and nutritious seasonal foods in whatever area we are in. I decided to try crab ramen in Yeosu. We bought a bag full for $3, put the crabs in a pot, and boiled them. The seller mentioned the name, but I forgot what it was. When the color of the crab shell turned red, I added the ramen, and the food was ready~!! Since I was cooking seafood, I only needed to add half the seasoning so it wouldn't be too salty. The soup was boiling and bubbled over. Ta-dah! The delicious crab ramen was complete!! The two of us had a great meal. Someday, I will try to cook this dish again when I go to Yeosu.

We decided to get a part-time job to fund the necessary finances. We knocked here and there, waiting for the door to open. At the same time, we sought God's will through early morning worship and QT to see if the path we were on was right. A month had already passed. At the early morning worship service on September 15, the word for that day was Ecclesiastes 7:15-18. "Whoever fears God will avoid extremes." The pastor said that if the navigation says to turn right after 500 meters ahead but you turn at 200 meters, you have to follow the directions after the navigator reroutes you. My husband told me that he thought we came to Yeosu too early. I had written this entry in my diary that day. "Then what should I do next? Should I go to another place in Jeollanam-do or to Seoul again?" I will have to pray. But how people would think and the thought that I had failed make my heart feel heavy.

And on September 23, when I wasn't accepted by the last job opening, the two of us went out for a drive to relieve our frustration. We went to Boseong, famous for green tea, and bought green tea ice cream to change our mood. While we were in the car again on the way back, a senior colleague called. "Why don't we work together again..." The next day we went to the early morning service as usual. On the way, I remembered the prophecy that instructor Esther had given me in South Africa during the afternoon tea time hosted by the Mozambique team. At the end of the paper she had filled out for me, she had written, "God's time is not my time." She said that all I had to do was get up every morning, praise God, and have a close relationship with God.

The passage from my quiet time that day was John 21:15-17. After denying Jesus, Peter was disappointed with himself. But when Jesus restored Peter and entrusted the ministry to his disciple again, what Jesus saw was not Peter's wisdom and power, but his love for Jesus. That morning, while quietly spending time in God's Word, I realized that it was not time yet for us to come to Yeosu. Just like when we had bought plane tickets to Brazil on the way to Israel earlier this year, we had not heard the voice of the Lord. This time, my heart's impatience was the problem. I realized that the timing was not right because I had gone too far ahead even though I was not ready. However, according to Esther's prophecy, God 's will is not according to my time but according to God's time. Just as Joseph tried to get out of prison through a cupbearer

(Genesis 40) but he waited two more years to lean on and trust God so I thought that this might be such a time for me.

Strangely however, unlike the time when we had bought tickets to Brazil, heartbreak and regret did not invade my heart. I was rather happy. I thought, *"I didn't hear the Lord's voice well, but why is my heart like this??"* Yet it was because I felt the warmth of the Lord. I felt that the Lord did not criticize us but accepted and blessed us even in spite of the mistakes we made from our impatience...Dongulee the car that my cousin gave us, our small group family who came down to Yeosu to support us, the friend who gifted us during Chuseok (Korean lunar thanksgiving), the house where I lived for two months, the piano teacher I met again by chance, and the senior pastor and wife of Yeosu First Presbyterian Church were all blessings that the Lord had sent to us. These blessings seemed like HE was saying to the child who made a mistake and failed, *"It's good that you have the courage to try ... It's okay, it's okay."* That morning I felt the Lord's kind and warm love.

My husband told me that just as Jesus came to Peter, who was working in his hometown (John 21), if we go back to Seoul to work and restore our love for Jesus, then Jesus will use us when the time comes ... After a while, I contacted the senior colleague who was waiting for my reply. It was written in my diary that day: "Leave myself in the hands of the all-powerful and good God. My soul, be at peace. Enjoy the time in Yeosu with Joshua during this time that God has given us. Thank you, God! I praise you, God!" And on the next day, I wrote down a list of the things I wanted to do in Yeosu before going to Seoul. "Go to Sado Island by boat, ride a bicycle on Odongdo Island, go to a German village on Namhae Island, and go to Pohang and Busan!" As usual, then and now, I still love having fun!

It was difficult waiting for the door to open, but we were very happy in Yeosu. During the two months there, we regained our health, and corrected our understanding of God's timing by meeting with mature believers. I once again felt the love of the Lord who turns even our mistakes into good. Thus, my husband and I returned to Seoul at the end of September 2014. Joseph and his wife welcomed us back and opened their home to us again. Thank you so much, friends! Within a month, we found a house near the hospital, and I started going to work in the first week of November. Meanwhile, my husband was the English pastor at a church. Our daily life in Seoul began again.

CHAPTER 31

From Faith to Faith

Korea, the city of Seoul, and my workplace. The place where I returned out of obedience to the Lord. However, returning wasn't as easy as I had thought. There were times when my self-esteem was deeply hurt, and there were times when I was angry enough to tear up; there were times when my heart was sorrowful, and there were times when I was happy and felt that working was worth it. Our daily life was a scene of intensity, a mixture of joy, anger, sorrow, and enjoyment.

One day at work, my head was down because I was upset. Then I remembered my outreach in South Africa. When Dr. Luke had examined me, he had said with a smile, "When God has you lay down your work and then has you do it again, you will be stronger than before." At that time, I had wondered what this meant, but when I came back to Korea, these words were a warm consolation and encouragement that the Lord had given me in advance through him. Whenever I felt low self-esteem and was overwhelmed, I remembered that this doctor had said to me with a smile, "You will be stronger than before." I took a deep breath and remembered my DTS. And I remembered the voice of the Lord, saying, "Because I love you, I let you have this trip." In this way, I engraved and carved my experiences from South Africa in my heart and was energized again.

There was once a time when no matter how hard I tried, my hurt heart didn't calm down. Anyway, I remember I was embarrassed for about two weeks. Then at some point

I could remember the voice of the Lord that I had heard while praying the Prayer House! The Lord had called me, "My jewel, my jewel." In response, I wanted to be a jewel that shines beautifully. When I was reminded of His voice, my mind was clear again as if a thick cloud was gone and a blue sky was coming, and I overcame this hardship. I don't even remember what happened now. Yes, a problem is just a problem. I think if a problem is resolved in the Lord, it will pass like the wind, and you won't even remember it. I agree with Solomon's statement in Ecclesiastes 5:20 which says, "They seldom reflect on the days of their life, because God keeps them occupied with goodness of hearts."

The journey from South Africa to the U.S. had passed by really fast, as if swept away by a strong wind. But this time, our time in Korea was not as "quick" as before. I hoped the cloud would rise quickly, but it didn't move. I realized that the obedience of the Israelites in Numbers 9, who obeyed and moved along with the clouds, was remarkable. You see, patience wasn't easy to learn. Furthermore, Joshua and I had just got out of the rose-colored honeymoon stage and had to learn a new way to love each other.

It has been five years since I came back to Korea. In the meantime, Joshua and I lost our baby, "our grape(our nickname for baby)," in the womb, and my husband suffered the pain of parting when his mother suddenly passed away. My husband also took a year off from his job because his health deteriorated due to overwork. I also repeatedly failed insemination and in-vitro procedures to have a baby. When these things weighed upon our hearts, and when the drought-like reality was longer than we thought, we had to work to be rooted deeper in the Lord while remembering the weakly rooted trees that had been uprooted by the wind in northern Sweden. But when it felt like we were passing through a long tunnel, God did not leave me or us alone. As Psalm 147:3 says, "The Lord heals the brokenhearted and binds up their wounds," He protected, comforted, and encouraged us. We learned how to love and comfort each other to the next level by receiving the love of the Lord. And I went down deeper growing the roots of faith. Dr. Luke had told Joshua and me to try a hobby, so we are riding bicycles together these days. While exercising, we look at the sky and at the quaint nature and birds around the neighborhood. My husband and I are building up happy memories and relieving stress. We are catching two birds with one stone. Riding our bicycles and looking at nature fits Joshua and me perfectly!!

Late August 2019. Today, my husband talked while riding his bicycle. It was the first anniversary of his mother's death. "A few days ago, I was blessed by the words from my morning devotion." "Really? Which verse was it?" "Romans 14:9. "For this very reason, Christ died and returned to life so that he might be the Lord of both the dead and the living." My mother died, but the Lord is still both Lord to my mother and me." When I heard this, I couldn't say anything. My heart was sad. But at the same time, I was relieved. My husband found comfort in the word of the Lord. And the Lord is holding my husband.

There were also painful memories of the miscarriage, but the Lord made it possible for me to have the wonderful experience of conceiving life. Now I naturally understand Psalm 139:14 "I praise you because I am fearfully and wonderfully made." I went through several trials of artificial insemination and test tube procedures, menopause symptoms experienced by sudden changes in hormones, shingles four times, and insomnia… It was a painful time for me, but it brought me closer to the Lord. In addition, I became more empathetic toward my patients when I saw them.

One day, a patient I was treating said, "Doctor, you look more comfortable than before." She was a person who used to come to me even before I did DTS. And about three years after I had rejoined the company, the nurses gave me a birthday card. It said, "Thank you for loving us." I used to be a nice doctor but, in some ways, I was also cold and sensitive. However, after DTS, I richly felt God's love, and I must have turned into a warmer person without realizing it. I remember when we had worshiped at the United Church in South Africa and Pastor Mary had preached from Jeremiah 18:1-4. In the same way, my character was being shaped like pottery made by the hand of God, the Potter.

In the meantime, we rebuilt the wall that had collapsed in our finances. It took more time than we thought, but now we have dealt with all the consequences of past poor financial management. Now, I am completely free from the debt which bound me for a long time. In doing so, we learned that we can experience miracles when we live according to Christian financial principles. I'm thankful to James for telling us to respect the Lord's natural laws. It was the advice we really needed. The Lord could miraculously have loosened the chains that were holding me, but He didn't. Instead, the Lord strengthened me to live by His natural laws and helped me to get rid of wrong financial values and habits. And I could break the chains that were binding me. Without the Lord's help, I had no strength to break the patterns of the past. He helped me face the present so that the past, which had become a trauma that I wanted to run away from, did not hold back my future. When I moaned because I was struggling, His heart also hurt, but the Lord patiently waited for me. I sincerely thank the Lord for giving me freedom.

Not only that. For us who wanted to do missionary work, the Lord opened the door for us to do missionary work in Seoul. That door was the English worship service at a church where my husband served (the church was located in front of a university). The service was attended by international students and workers from as many as 17 countries! We were able to worship the Lord every week with people from so many different places such as Southeast Asia, China, India, Africa, Europe, North America, and even South America, where we had not been yet. Those were really precious times. The grace of the Lord is deep and wide!!

What did DTS mean to me? It is insufficient to describe it as a special lecture to move away from everyday life and learn about God-there is something more. Through DTS, I felt deeply God's love for me. That's why DTS became a turning point in my life. During the lectures, outreach, and our voyage from Sweden to Israel to Kansas City, I learned about the Lord, my relationship with Him, listening to His voice, and how to live by faith. It was a really special time.

However, even after DTS, God's lessons of love continued. It was putting what I learned into action even if there were no special events, no staff to help, and no classmates to encourage one another; and I was just living out my daily life. It was the process of applying the new program downloaded from the Lord. Even at this time, God's love continued. So I was able to remember what DTS taught me and apply it to work in my life. This must be why the instructors consistently emphasized intimacy with God so that I could continue to grow in the faith that the Lord is still with me, loves me, and guides me in my daily life in Seoul, Korea.

Before and after DTS, we experienced the Lord's guidance dramatically, but for the past five years, it seems that we have lived by relying on the detailed voice of the Lord. After coming back to Korea, we were facing the wind storms that passed by. But the Lord holds us up so that we don't fall even if we are shaken. I am so grateful to the Lord. We are still learning who the Lord is and who we are in our daily routine. We hope that the Lord will lead us deeper. Just as the water from the temple rises to the ankles, knees, and waist, and swells more and more so that one can swim in the water. Like Ezekiel 47. The Lord takes me gently, step by step.

Joyfully and freely in the river of the Holy Spirit. From faith to faith...

True Freedom

Freedom in the Spirit
He drew near first
Who God is and who I am?

My life's vision coming anew
Throwing off perspectives of the past
All things becoming new

Changing me, changing my life
Not a self-centered but a Christ-centered love
This change by His Grace

Where there is the Spirit of the Lord
There is freedom (2 Corinthians 3:17)

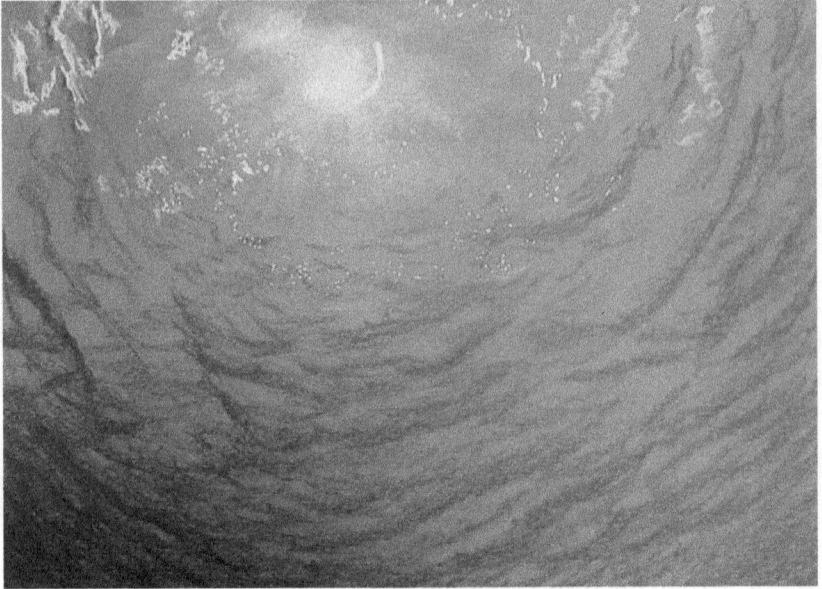
Fig 11. Joyful and Free in the river of Holy Spirit

Epilogue

Dec 27, 2019 Where is the Dream Team five years later?

- **Casablanca (Dream Team intercessor)**

She raised employees at work who confessed, "I want to believe in the God that you serve." She is working hard today! She is gentle and humorous, and she has a special ability to evangelize to people naturally. Like a hunting dog that does not let go, she is persistent in her passion for salvation. In that respect, Casablanca is the Lord's Jindo-dog(an intelligent, royal, and very courageous Korean dog). She transferred to the Graduate School Youth Counseling Department and is preparing for her second life by working with both office workers and students. Go, Casablanca!!

- **Sungeun (Dream Team intercessor)**

She met her future husband in front of the church restaurant. His ideal type was a woman who prayed like Hannah and served like Lydia. They got married with the blessing of the Dream Team and church leaders. After two years of being newlyweds, they received long-term missionary training and were sent to Country C in early 2019. She sends reports on their mission with prayer letters~

- **Sukyung (Dream Team hair care leader)**

After 30 years of teaching, she was admitted to the Kona DTS in April 2019, shouting the motto, "In my second act, I want to live by following the voice of the Lord." She returned after completing her outreach in Papua New Guinea. Sukyung and the people around her are thrilled with anticipation at how the Lord will lead her in the future.

- **Sookhyun (Dream Team dentist)**

She went to be with the Lord in January 2018 after terminal ovarian cancer was discovered during her missionary training. She impressed us with her passion for missions until the day of her death. Dear Sister ~ Thank you. We miss you!!

- **Joseph & his wife (Past Dream Team leader & general affairs)**

They work hard at their respective workplaces on the weekdays and at church on the weekends. They intercede with a special heart for Korea and the Korean people. Their passion is a hot furnace!

- **Jiwon (Dream Team secretary)**

The answer to her prayer for the ministry of the Dream Team is, "Keep going". In the end, she helped the next two Dream Team leaders and is still working hard as the team secretary. While I wrote this book, she went on the Dream Team Nepal outreach with her older sister, my best friend Misun, and returned.

- **Joshua & I (Dream Team barber & dermatologist)**

My husband is an English pastor at a church near a university. I am a housewife, a part-time doctor during the week, and a pastor's wife on the weekends~

And not long ago...

I found out that a new road was opened on the long course that I had dreamed of five years ago. Again, like the time five years ago, our new journey started one day. But this time, unlike last time, the journey started with my husband. One day my husband told me. "I wanna go home..." I was surprised by his sudden words, but when I heard his words, I immediately thought that these words are not to be overlooked.

In fact, for the next step after the English worship service that my husband has been in charge of for the past three years, I had been preparing my heart since early 2019. However, America was somewhere I hadn't even thought of going for our next step. I had thought that we would maybe go to Ilsan which is north of Seoul... *Was my husband like this when I said let's go to DTS?!* Anyway, this time, my husband and I prayed together and did our morning devotions and waited for the Lord's confirmation. The words I read every day kept saying that going to America was right. But my heart hesitated. Then one day, while I was taking a break from work, I looked out the window from my office room and prayed to God. "God! Couldn't it be that my husband misheard Your voice? Could he have misunderstood?"

Then I sat down again, calmed down, and started doing my devotion, which I couldn't do this morning because I was busy. 1 Peter 3:1 "Wives, in the same way submit yourselves to your own husbands." *Ugh!!! Why is this the verse today of all days...* It was the verse about Sarah's daughters that had struck me and that I had meditated on since receiving it in South Africa. That is how I ended the conflict in my heart on that day, obeyed the command to submit to my husband, and started preparing to go to my husband's town in the Northwestern United States.

I have anticipation for the future that the Lord will lead us. However, at the same time, I feel sad that I have to leave my beloved place and say good-bye to my loved ones. The Lord has been giving us the words from Philippians 4:13, "I can do all things through him who gives me strength." for the past one to two weeks. Yes! With the Lord, my anxiety about the future gradually turns into anticipation, and my eyes begin to sparkle with hope. A new voyage is about to begin again soon. We raise our sails to the blowing wind and are sailing again today following the wind from the Lord~

Sailboat

Deep blue sea
Crashing waves
When we're struggling with headwinds
He walks over the water

Glittering blue sea
Cutting through the waves
When we're excited by the fair wind
He blows the wind on the mast

Let's spread the sails vigorously
To the sea of hope
Today is also
Amazing Grace

Fig 12. The start of a new voyage (Wood Engraving)!!

About The Author

Heejin Han Kimjacobs was born and raised in South Korea. While she was contemplating during her youth what to do, she was so impressed as she read her Bible by the stories of Jesus healing the sick that she decided to become a doctor. She experienced the Lord's miraculous help whenever she went through difficult hurdles in the process of going to medical school and becoming a dermatologist. In 2013 she did DTS in Worcester, South Africa with her husband. Through DTS, she richly felt God's kind and gentle love. She was an associate staff member at YWAM -AIIM Pneuma Springs, and during this time, she and her husband lived in Monroe, Washington, USA. Currently, she and her husband are pioneering the YWAM-AIIM(Antioch Institute for International Ministries) Yeosu base in Yeosu, Jeollanam-do, South Korea.

www.ingramcontent.com/pod-product-compliance
Lightning Source LLC
Chambersburg PA
CBHW060317050426
42449CB00011B/2525